CLOSE YOUR
VOLUME 2

PUT SERVICE
BACK INTO THE
CHURCH SERVICE

MAKING YOUR CHURCH SERVICE LOOK MORE LIKE JESUS

JEREMY MYERS

Put Service Back into the Church Service
Making Your Church Service Look More Like Jesus
© 2013, 2018 by Jeremy Myers

Published by Redeeming Press
Dallas, OR 97338
RedeemingPress.com

Learn more about Jeremy Myers by visiting RedeemingGod.com

Library of Congress Cataloging-in-Publication Data

Myers, Jeremy, 1975-
    Put Service Back into the Church Service:
    Making Your Church Service Look More Like Jesus / Jeremy Myers.
    p. cm.
    ISBN: 978-1-939992-05-5 (Paper)
    ISBN: 978-1-939992-06-2 (Mobi)
    ISBN: 978-1-939992-07-9 (ePub)
    1. Church 2. Ecclesiology 3. Mission 4. Myers, Jeremy, 1975-. I. Title

---

JOIN JEREMY MYERS AND LEARN MORE
Take Bible and theology courses by joining Jeremy at
RedeemingGod.com/join/

Receive updates about free books, discounted books,
and new books by joining Jeremy at
RedeemingGod.com/reader-group/

TAKE THE
SKELETON CHURCH
ONLINE COURSE

Join others at
RedeemingGod.com/join/
and get all my courses for free, including
"The Skeleton Church" online course:

GET EBOOKS AND THEOLOGY COURSES AT
REDEEMINGGOD.COM/JOIN/

Thanks for reading!

Books in the *Close Your Church for Good* Series

Books in the *Christian Questions* Series

Other Books by Jeremy Myers

All books are available at Amazon.com
Learn about each title at the end of this book

For Sam,
who taught me that church could
truly look like Jesus

TABLE OF CONTENTS

INTRODUCTION

Churches around the world are trying to revitalize their church services. In the past, their attempts at doing so were limited to having a revival service, bringing in a dynamic guest speaker, switching up the preaching style, or putting some drums on the stage. But when these changes lost their novelty, churches had to up the ante and do something more extreme to grab the attention of visitors and attract people to their Sunday morning service. Some churches went "Vegas style" and gave away an H2 Hummer. Other churches decided to go *au natural* and moved their church service outside among the birds and the trees by building huge amphitheaters complete with running streams and grassy hillsides. A few went Amish style and did away with electricity so they could worship by candlelight. Others went the opposite direction and added stage lights, spotlights, fog machines, and a state-of-the-art sound system. Many churches believed that multi-million dollar additions and church renovations were the key to reaching people for Christ, with each church trying to outdo the other in opulence and beauty. One famous mega church in Dallas, Texas recently spent over $130 million on construction, remodeling, and renovation.

Some days, it seems there is almost nothing churches will not try … unless it is the one thing they should have tried.

Few churches have tried to look more like Jesus.

Though this short book does not provide all the answers to helping the church look more like Jesus, it does provide two suggestions for helping churches take a step in the right direction. There are two things that most traditional churches have, which are major roadblocks and hindrances to looking like Jesus. They are the church service and the church programs.

Though both of these activities are created and produced with the intention of serving people, we may find that true service only begins once we cancel the church service and cut the church programs. By putting service back into the church service and focusing on people rather than programs, the church can begin to once again look like Jesus in the world.

CHAPTER 1

CANCEL YOUR CHURCH SERVICE

"It is not scientific doubt, not atheism, not pantheism, not agnosticism, that in our day and in this land is likely to quench the light of the gospel. It is a proud, sensuous, selfish, luxuriant, church-going, hollow-hearted prosperity." —Frederic Huntington

It is extremely odd that in the thinking of most of today's Christians, the primary factor setting apart true and faithful followers of Jesus from backslidden apostates is whether or not a person attends a Sunday morning church service.

I remember having many conversations as a pastor with people who had stopped going to church. I tried to convince them that if they truly loved Jesus and were really intent on serving Him, they needed to return to the church and attend the Sunday morning service on a regular basis. When they did not return, I remember talking with my elders about whether or not we should remove the wayward people from our membership rolls and which of us should try to convince these people of the error of their ways. It wasn't so bad if a person was attending a home church, but if someone was attending no church, they had clearly fallen away from the faith. In one of these discussions, I remember one elder quoting 1 John 2:19. "They went out from us, but they did not really belong to us. For if they had belonged to us, they would have remained with us; but their going showed that none of them belonged to us" (NIV). In other words, their departure proved their apostasy.

So I find it ironic that I myself have "left the church." At least, that is what many people think. I no longer attend a Sunday morning church service, and so this means, in the minds of many, that I have departed from the faith, have fallen away, and am living in a backslidden condition.

Yet I have never been so close to Jesus. I have never loved and served people more. I have never been more involved in the lives of people who need love, encouragement, healing, service, and friendship. I have never seen more answers to prayer. I have never been more in tune to the leading and direction of the Holy Spirit. I have never seen the Scriptures come alive to me in the way they do now. I have never before seen God's hand so clearly at work in my life, leading and directing me in His ways. I have never had more conversations with people about Jesus and Scripture than I do now. But in the eyes of many, because I no longer attend a Sunday morning church service, I am a sinful, backslidden, carnal Christian.

Isn't this odd? In today's church culture, you can serve people in the name of Jesus, exhibit great faith, hope, and love toward God and others, meditate daily upon God's Word, and practice God's constant presence through prayer and fellowship, and yet if you are not "attending a church," many church-going Christians will think you are not truly following Jesus. On the other hand, if none of these things are true, but you sit in a pew for 90 minutes on Sunday morning, then many church-going Christians will think you are doing just fine in your walk with God. This is especially true if you are one of the "faithful few" who not only attends the Sunday morning worship service but also shows up for a Wednesday night Bible study or prayer meeting.

Something has gone seriously wrong in Christianity if following Jesus consists primarily in showing up at certain events in certain buildings at certain times of the week.

I know the objections to this idea. As a pastor I taught it all myself. It is in the church service where teaching, encouragement, and instruction take place. It is on Sunday morning that we fellowship, learn, and worship. It is there that we receive guidance and counsel. It is at this time that our batteries are recharged so we can go out and love on the world. We gather so we can scatter. It is in the service where we put our spiritual gifts into practice. The church service is where we minister to one another.

These are the things we say, but are they true? Could it not be just as true that these are the arguments we use to support the man-made edifice of the "church service"? Is it possible that although Jesus is calling people to Himself, many of us in leadership call people to an event? Have we ever thought that while Jesus wants people to follow Him into the world, we want people to follow us out of the world and into a building?

BOTH-AND VS. EITHER-OR

"No, no!" you say. "You are making a false dichotomy. It isn't either-or; it is both-and. We don't have to choose between following Jesus and going to church; people can do both. In fact, going to church *helps* people follow Jesus."

Yes, that may be true. I do not deny it. I know that for millions of people around the world and throughout the last 1,700 years, attending a church service on a Sunday morning has been a vital part of their life in Christ, their fellowship with the saints, and their source of encouragement from God and instruction in the Word. Attending church (and pastoring a church) was exactly this for most of my life and could be again.

The problem arises when the "both-and" experience of *both* attending church *and* following Jesus into the world becomes "either-or" and we tell the people with our words or our actions that if they have to choose between one or the other, the most important thing is attending church. We may not say it this way, but we model it, imply it, and encourage it. If a neighbor has car problems on Sunday morning, people believe it is more important to get to church than to help their neighbor. If a coworker calls late on Saturday night, says that her husband just left, and asks if the two of you could meet to talk on Sunday morning, you would likely ask her to wait until Sunday afternoon because you have to go to church. At least, this is what many church-going Christians would tell her.

The bottom line is this. We pay lip service to the idea that attending a church service *helps* us follow Jesus into the world. However, the sad reality is that far too often and for most people, attending a church service can actually *get in the way* of following Jesus.

Let me put it another way. If your Sunday morning routine of getting up, getting breakfast, getting the kids ready for church, getting out the door, and getting to church on time is anything like that of most churchgoers, then you know that Sunday morning can be one of the most hectic times of the week. It is when we fight with our spouses the most. It is when the kids most frequently misbehave. It is when the call comes in from the friend who just found out he has cancer. Or we receive a text from an extended family member in need of help. Or it has been raining all week and it is finally sunny on Sunday, and some friends invite us to join them at the lake. Why do these things always happen on Sunday?

I used to think it was the devil trying to keep me from going to church. But now I think it may be Jesus saying, "Don't go to church today. Instead, follow Me into the world. Let's go work on your marriage with your spouse. Let's go spend time with a family member in need. Let's go help your neighbor with her lawn. Let's go enjoy life with your friends." These are not temptations from the devil, but invitations from Jesus to go where He goes and do what He does. He invites us to these things on Sunday mornings because He knows that although going to church can sometimes be a "both-and," we more often than not make it an "either-or," and choose going to church over following Jesus. So Jesus orchestrates these decisions on Sunday morning, giving us an opportunity to choose Him over going to church.

The sooner pastors and church leaders recognize this, the better. If we recognize this, then we can encourage the people in our congregations that if there is a choice between following Jesus into the world and coming to church for singing songs and hearing a sermon, they should choose Jesus every time. We will talk about how to do that in the rest of this chapter, but first, we must face the primary objection to this idea.

When most church leaders and churchgoers hear the idea that we do not need to go to church in order to follow Jesus, they object by saying something along the following lines: "But doesn't Jesus *want* us to go to church? Do not the Scriptures command it? When we choose church over the other things in life, are we not doing this out of obedience to God and His Word? Doesn't the Bible say that we should not forsake the assembling of ourselves together?"

These are good questions. Let's deal first with what Scripture says about attending church.

DO NOT FORSAKE THE ASSEMBLING

It must be pointed out that the Bible nowhere calls people to "attend church" or "go to church." As has been pointed out *ad nauseam* by numerous other authors and teachers, Jesus did not call us to *go to church* but to *be the church*. Church is not a place we can go; it is something we are. As I argued in my book *Skeleton Church,* the church is the people of God who follow Jesus into the world.[1] This means that we do not go to church; the church goes with us.

Yet generally, when someone suggests that Christians don't need to attend church, a pastor or other church leader is quick to

---

[1] Jeremy Myers, *Skeleton Church: The Bare Bones Definition of Church* (Dallas, OR: Redeeming Press, 2012).

quote Hebrews 10:25. This verse warns believers against forsaking the assembling of themselves together. But let's be clear. Not only does this verse say nothing about "church," it says nothing about how often believers should meet, where they should meet, or with whom. Nor does the text state what should be done when they meet. All it says is that they should continue to meet and should encourage one another when they do so.

Beyond this, however, there is something even more interesting about this text. It is questionable whether the passage can directly be applied to believers today since the original recipients of the letter were former Jews who were now being pressured through persecution to return to the customs and laws of Judaism. The word that the author uses in Hebrews 10:25 for "assembling together" is *episunagōgē*, which could possibly be an allusion to the Jewish synagogue. Maybe the author is telling his readers that even though they face persecution at the synagogue, they should continue to attend the Jewish synagogue.

Of course, it is also likely that these Jewish believers in Jesus had started their own "Christian synagogue" patterned after the Jewish traditions, and it was this they should not abandon, even in the face of persecution (cf. Jas 2:2; 5:14). If either of these theories are true, we must be careful about using the verse to guilt people into "coming to church." The Jewish synagogue that the author might have had in mind would have met on Saturdays and would have been much different from anything we think of as "church" today.

Nevertheless, I do not believe the verse is referring to a Jewish synagogue. The word used in Hebrews 10:25 is also used in 2 Thessalonians 2:1 where Paul is writing about the ingathering of believers for the Day of the Lord, after which time we will spend eternity with Jesus. Many take the term in 2 Thessalonians 2:1 as a reference to the rapture, but this is not necessarily the best understanding. Instead, this word (like the term for "church," *ekklēsia*) does not refer to a time and place where believers gather together on a regular basis for singing and sermons.

Rather, it refers to the *activity of God* in gathering together a people for Himself to accomplish His will on earth. We are His hands and feet—His Body—on earth, *gathered together (episunagōgē)* by God to love and serve those around us, just like Jesus. This gathering is not primarily an assembly in a physical location at a regular timeslot during the week, but is a spiritual gathering of believers from every tongue, tribe, and nation over all the earth. Jesus wants His gospel to spread over all the earth and so He has gathered people together from all over the earth to be His witnesses. In light of this, both 2 Thessalonians 2:1 and Hebrews 10:25 remind believers that God has gathered the church out of the world for a purpose. The warning in both texts is that some people are in the habit of forsaking this purpose, which is what we must not do.

So what does Hebrews 10:25 teach? It is telling believers to fulfill their God-given purpose and encourage others to do the same. And what is this purpose? Each person has their own unique purpose in God's plan, but the overarching purpose of the spiritual assembly of God is to live life and love others like Jesus. Is sitting in a building for two hours on Sunday morning the best way to accomplish this purpose? This activity may be helpful for some, but it may not be helpful for others. To allow people to fulfill their purpose, we must set them free from the manmade requirement of "attending church." While it is fine for people to "attend church" if they find it helpful in fulfilling their God-given purpose on earth, we must also grant people the freedom to not "attend church" if they do not find this activity helpful for following Jesus into the world and loving others like Jesus.

OUT OF CONTROL CHURCH

Giving people the liberty to choose whether or not they "attend church" is a terrifying idea for many pastors and church leaders. It is a scary thought because we depend on the people to fill the pews and pay the bills—one of which is our own salary. But what if the church didn't have buildings or paid pastors? Would we then feel free to let our people go? The answer by most pastors would still be "No." We not only need people to pay the bills of the church building and church staffing, but more than that, we feel responsible to protect the people God has put under our care. We believe it is our task to help them know what to believe and how to live. Without vision the people perish (Prov 29:18), and without leaders the church spins out of control.

As a former pastor myself, that is how I thought. I viewed the relationship between the people in the pew and the pastor in the pulpit as mutually beneficial. The people should attend services and give of their time and money to support the budget and programs of the church. In return, I would do my best to provide for their spiritual needs and guide them through the hazards of life. I could quote numerous Scripture passages in my defense. Jesus told Peter to "feed my sheep" (John 21:15-19), and Peter later passed this instruction on to the elders in the church when he told them to "shepherd the flock of God" (1 Pet 5:2). Paul told Timothy to "preach the Word" (2 Tim 4:2) and that elders are worthy of a double honor (1 Tim 5:17).

Looking back, especially at some of the disputes I had with certain people and some of the struggles and problems we faced as a church, I now believe that my ultimate concern was for my own prominence and power. I am not saying this is true of every pastor, but it was true of me. I have come to realize that when it came to the people "under my care," I wanted to control them. I thought that if they believed what I taught and did what I said, everybody's life (including mine) would be better. I also believed that greater attendance on Sunday morning would provide greater power, prominence, and influence for the church (and myself) in the wider community, which would help advance the Kingdom of God. I even remember watching some of the internal feuds of other local churches, hoping that some of their people would leave and start attending my church.

Most pastors, I believe, have good hearts. Looking back at my own pastoral ministry, I do not think I was *trying* to manipulate people or control their lives. But I honestly believed (as many pastors do) that since I had the spiritual gift of Pastor-Teacher, it was my job to shepherd the people, guide their lives, teach them how to live, and give them the direction they needed. I failed to recognize that while the spiritual gift of Pastor-Teacher does include the concepts of instruction and exhortation, there is a fine line between *tending* others and *controlling* others. There is a delicate balance between providing insight into Scripture and making our understanding of Scripture equivalent with Scripture itself.

What often ends up happening in pastoral ministry is that the pastor sets himself up as the spiritual head of the church, thereby usurping the role that should be reserved for Jesus Christ alone. When this happens, we get offended when people do not follow our advice. We become angry when they disagree with our opinion. We become unhappy and dissatisfied when we are not paid enough or praised enough. These sorts of attitudes do not reveal a heart focused on incarnational living according to the principles of the Kingdom of God, but rather reveal a heart focused on satanic influences of power, prestige, recognition, manipulation, and control. Though I did not recognize it at the time, now that I have left pastoral ministry, I fully confess that these were characteristics in my heart and life when I was a pastor. In many ways, I still struggle with these issues today.

I do not pretend to know the hearts and minds of all pastors and church leaders around the world and throughout time. But from my own observation and from my reading of church history, it seems that my experience is not unique. Generally, our motives are sound; we truly want to help people. But many of us believe deep down in the core of our being that the best way to help people is to control them. We believe, due to our pastoral experience and knowledge of the Scriptures, that we know what is right and best. And if people will just do what we say, everybody will live in peace and harmony.

So how do we get people to know what to believe, learn how to live, and practice the things they should do? It's easy: We bring them all into a room and tell them. We get them to "come to church" on Sunday morning. We encourage their faithful attendance, and we tell them how to behave and what to believe. The Sunday morning church service is the best and easiest way to control the lives of other people.

If you are a pastor or church leader, these sorts of suggestions are probably upsetting. Please understand that I am not trying to condemn or criticize. I believe that your motives are pure and you only have people's best interests at heart. It is undoubtedly true that you are only concerned about your God-given task of watching over the people whom He has placed under your care. You only want to teach and guide them so that they can live the best life possible as followers of Jesus.

But if you are like most pastors, somewhere along the way of teaching and helping people, the desire to control the beliefs and behaviors of others crept in and usurped your good intentions. If you do not believe this, it is easy to find out if it is true of you. To assess your own heart in this matter, all you have to do is look at what feelings emerge when it is suggested that you cancel your Sunday service.

If someone came up to you after the church service on Sunday and said, "Pastor, I think we should cancel our Sunday Services from now on," what would your reaction be? What would you say in response? What would you think about the person who said this? What thoughts would pop into your mind? Would you object? Are there any fears? If so, what are they?

Most pastors believe that if they canceled the Sunday morning church service, this would be the end of their church and the end of their paycheck. Most pastors believe that if a person wants church services to cease, it is only because the person is backslidden in their faith or wants to live selfishly. Most pastors believe that without the weekly Sunday service to recharge people's spirits and remind them of what to believe and how to behave, most people will quickly fall away from Jesus and drop off into sinful habits and wicked ways. Most pastors believe that the church service is what holds the church together and keeps Christianity moving forward.

Yet none of this is true, except for possibly the part about the pastor losing his job. But is that the only reason we have church services? So that pastors can have jobs? Of course not. Upon careful introspection, however, it seems that rather than providing encouragement and exhortation to the people who attend church, the real reason for holding Sunday morning services is a desire for power, prominence, and control.

We *tell* people that the church service is about encouragement and edification, but this is not really true. This is simply something we have been telling ourselves for so long, we have come to believe it. Though people may get *some* encouragement and instruction from church services, there are numerous more effective means than sitting in rows for an hour or two while we sing a few songs together, bow our heads respectfully while someone prays, and listen to someone give a talk about something the Lord "laid on his heart."

If we really wanted to encourage and edify people, we would cancel the church service and do something more effective. The fact that we keep the church service going means that we either don't know about the numerous other more effective ways, or that despite all our claims, mutual encouragement and edification are not the true purpose of modern church services. I suspect it is the latter. Though church leaders often say that Christians are to gather for edification and encouragement, this is not what the true purpose of the typical Sunday morning church service.

What then is the real purpose? The real purpose for church services reveals itself when we challenge their existence. The true purpose becomes obvious when the practice of the church service is questioned or challenged. When someone suggests that church services cease, pastors get upset, church leaders get angry, fingers get pointed, and people get labeled as heretics and apostates. These sorts of reactions suggest that the real reason for church services has something to do with power over people, prominence in the eyes of others, and control over beliefs and behaviors. So no matter what the cost, no matter how time-intensive or financially expensive, we keep the church services going.

It is time for pastors and church leaders to practice what we preach. It is time to give back to people the freedom they have in Christ to follow wherever He leads, and the flexibility offered by grace to do whatever they believe God wants. It is time for pastors and church leaders to realize that it is not we who are the head of the church, but Jesus Christ alone, and it is not we who guide and empower people for Christlike living, but the Holy Spirit who indwells each believer. It is time to give up our quest for power, to discard our desire for prestige, and to abandon our pursuit of prominence. It is time to stop trying to control people.

We can start by canceling our church services.

EXIT SIGNS

Practically speaking, canceling the church service is a wise move. People are leaving the church in droves. According to numerous recent studies, less than 20% of people in the United States regularly attend church, and of those who do, 2.7 million more leave the church annually. These numbers are vastly different in other countries, and especially in third-world countries where conversion numbers are exponentially rising. Here in the United States, however, the combined membership of all Protestant denominations declined by almost 5 million people in the last ten years, while the US population increased by 24 million during the same time period.[2] The church is declining in numbers even as the population numbers expand. And it's not just attendance. Exit signs are everywhere. Conversions, baptisms, membership, retention, participation, giving, religious literacy, and effect on culture are all down across the board.[3]

Prominent pastors and church leaders suggest various reasons for this widespread decline and propose numerous solutions for reversing this trend. Some of these proposed solutions are why we see churches embracing new ways of doing church, new service structures, and new methods of attracting members. The thinking is that people are bored, apathetic, or disillusioned with church, and if we can find ways to grab their attention, keep them entertained, and show them how the church is relevant for their lives, they will come back and get involved once again.

But I am convinced that this is another example where we have missed the forest for the trees. People are not bored, apathetic, or disillusioned. It is not that people don't care about God or

---

[2] These numbers come from the U.S. Census Bureau, and they have been independently confirmed by parallel studies from organizations like the Institute of Church Leadership Development, LifeWay Research, the Southern Baptist Convention, and the Assemblies of God.

[3] Christine Wicker, *The Fall of the Evangelical Nation: The Surprising Crisis Inside the Church* (New York: HarperOne, 2008), ix.

serving others. People do not leave the church to become atheists. No, most people who leave the church do so because they have discovered that they can follow Jesus, love other people, and serve God *better* outside the four walls of traditional "churchianity" than within. People do not leave church because they do not love God or do not want to serve people. They leave church because they do love God and want to serve people, and they find that attending church often gets in the way of such things.

George Barna, in his book *Revolution,* indicates that involvement in traditional "brick and mortar" churches is declining. At the same time, his research shows that the number of people who are committed to following Jesus in their lives, at their jobs, and among their friends is expanding exponentially.[4] If Barna is right, the church is not dying. For those who have eyes to see what God is doing, His church has never looked better! People stop attending church, not because they are rebelling against God, but because *as a faithful member of the church*, they *are* following God. People want to love others like Jesus, and for whatever reason, sitting in a particular building at a certain time of the week hinders their ability to love and serve others in the way they feel Jesus is calling them.

Pastors and church leaders should not fight against this but should rejoice in it. We should celebrate the fact that people want to follow Jesus into the world by loving and serving others. Their departure from our church services should not be viewed as a threat but as a blessing. It should be viewed as another step in the

[4] George Barna, *Revolution* (Wheaton: Tyndale, 2006).

life of faith. When people leave the church building to be the church in the world, it is a beautiful expression of the worldwide movement of the Holy Spirit upon God's people as the gospel expands the Kingdom of God around the earth.

This is why giving people permission to leave church is so important (many will eventually leave anyway). Since many people are thinking of leaving, why not shock the socks off them and tell them not to come! Rather than make them sneak out the door, rather than making them feel guilty for not attending church, rather than forcing them to come up with lame excuses as to why they "missed church," why not show them the door by giving them permission to follow Jesus *wherever* He leads, even if it is away from the Sunday morning church service?

In fact, once we think about it, "missing church" and "attending church" should not even be in the church's vocabulary. Such terminology reveals a tendency to view church as a function and a place, rather than the people of God who follow Jesus into the world. If we really want to help the people of God follow Jesus out into the world, we need to put up big EXIT signs on all our doors and lead people out of the building in which they are trapped. We need to send them out into the world where God can work in them and through them to bring light, love, and hope to the hurting people all around. If people are exiting the church building anyway, the role of the pastor and church leader is not to block them or condemn them, but to bless them and guide them on their way. Let's invite people into the adventure of loving God and loving others outside the brick walls and stained glass of a church building.

One way we can show the people we are serious about this is

by canceling the church service.

GO TO CHURCH AND SIN

There is another reason to cancel the church service. If we fail to give people the freedom to follow Jesus into the world and instead try to keep them within the four walls of our buildings, forcing them to do what we think is true worship and true service, this may very well cause the church service itself to become sinful. Modern Christians are not the only ones who have met together in large groups to worship God, pray, sing songs, and listen to teaching from the Bible. God's people have been doing this for thousands of years. And God isn't necessarily opposed to it, unless it gets in the way of certain things that are nearest and dearest to the heart of God. What are these things?

If we take passages like Isaiah 1:12-13, Amos 4:4-5, Amos 5:21-24, Jeremiah 14:12, Hosea 6:6, and Micah 6:6-8, and put them together with modern terminology, we could say that the following is what God thinks about the church service:

"Go to church and sin!
Attend Bible studies and multiply your sins!
Volunteer to clean the church.
Faithfully tithe your 10%.
Praise Jesus for all He has given you.
Thank God for your many blessings.
For these are the things, Oh Christian, you love to do,"
says the LORD God.

"I hate your pot lucks.
Nor do I delight in your Christian concerts.
Though you give generously to the building fund,
And donate faithfully to Christian organizations,
I will not even look at these many gifts.

"Cease your many sermons,
Stop writing your faithful blog.
Get out of your pew,
Put away all your Christian books.

"When you fast, I will not listen.
Though you cry out, I will not hear.
I will not accept your offerings
And sacrifices of praise.

"Take away from me the noise of your many songs,
Your numerous prayers are an abomination!
Quit playing the guitars, banging on the drums,
And raising your hands in praise.
Stop trampling the parking lots
In your eagerness to get to church.

"Sunday morning, Sunday night.
Wednesday evening, Friday morning.
I hate all your meetings.
I despise your numerous studies.
They are all evil in my sight.

"Instead, let justice roll down like a waterfall,
And righteousness like an ever-flowing stream.
I desire mercy, not sacrifice.
I want you to do justice, love kindness,
And walk humbly with your God."

Does this sound harsh? It probably sounded so to the Israelites who heard God say such things about their temple worship, yearly festivals, frequent fasts, and sacrificial system, much of which He instituted! Notice however, that it is not that God doesn't desire such things; it is that these things were supposed to lead to something else. The worship of God is supposed to result in justice, kindness, and the humble service of others. If our church services are not accomplishing this (and preaching about such topics is not enough), we should cancel our services until we have set our priorities straight. After all, despite all we say and despite what we know to be true, the top priority of many churches boils down to filling the pews on Sunday morning. We have attendance dependence.

ATTENDANCE DEPENDENCE

Although everybody knows that filling the pews on Sunday morning is not the top priority of church, we nevertheless imply that it is. Pastors live and die by the Sunday morning numbers. When pastors attend conferences, one topic of conversation is nearly always about how large their churches are and how they can add more numbers to their Sunday attendance. During the year, pastors preach sermons about the importance of attending church. In church membership classes, we include the idea that attendance is one of the primary responsibilities of membership and a key ingredient of true discipleship. Whenever you miss a Sunday or two, you will usually get calls from concerned friends and family because they didn't see you "in church." You may even get a letter from the pastor letting you know you were missed, and this letter will nearly always reiterate the necessity of attending church for our spiritual well-being. If you fail to attend for a month or longer, rumors will begin to be spread that you have "backslidden" or have "abandoned the faith."

This emphasis on church attendance has resulted in three troubling tendencies. First, there are those who believe that if they attend church on Sunday morning, they have fulfilled what God wants. In one church I pastored, I asked a talented and gifted lady to consider helping out for a weekday community outreach we had planned. She had faithfully attended the church for a few years, but she never came to any activity beyond Sunday morning, so I invited her to get more involved.

Her answer floored me. She said, "Pastor, I come to church every Sunday. I am there on time. I sit and sing the songs. I listen to the sermon. I tithe 10%. Thank you for asking me to help with this outreach, but I believe that when I walk out those doors on Sunday morning, I have completed my religious duty for the week." Though we rarely hear it stated this bluntly, this belief is more widespread than we imagine. But such a mentality is largely due to the frequent reminders by the pastor and other church staff that church attendance is critical to following Jesus.

Second, this constant emphasis on church attendance can also lead to the other extreme, where people become addicted to attending church. For some, church attendance is an idol whereby they measure the spiritual maturity of themselves and others. If church attendance is critical for following Jesus, then logically, the more you attend church, the better follower you are. So they attend Sunday morning, Sunday night, the Wednesday prayer meeting, the Thursday night cell group, and the Saturday morning men's breakfast.

Finally, the emphasis on church attendance can lead to the problem of church attendance being viewed as the epitome of Christian faithfulness. Your life may be in shambles, but if you show up for the Sunday morning church services, most Christians will think you are doing okay in your Christian walk. As long as Christians show up on Sunday morning, nobody really cares too much how your relationship with God is during the rest of the week, or how you treat your neighbors, behave toward your family, or interact with coworkers at your job. Your life could be full of greed, lust, profanity, anger, malice, and deceit, with no love for God or for other people, but if you show up at a church service on Sunday morning, people assume that things are going okay and you are making progress on the path of discipleship.

These kinds of churchgoers—those who fulfill their weekly duty by attending the Sunday morning service, those who gorge themselves on a weekly smorgasbord of services, Bible studies, and prayer meetings, and those who use church services to hide who they really are—all have the same problem. They suffer from attendance dependence. They depend on church attendance to keep them spiritually healthy or as an indication that they *are* healthy. They all think that attending church fulfills their responsibility to God, to the pastor, to each other, and to the lost and dying world, and that as long as they show up for at least one service on Sunday morning, they are fulfilling God's will and doing what Jesus expects from His followers.

PUSHER PASTORS

Tragically, this attendance dependence is not usually the fault of the people in the pews. No, it is usually the pastors who either imply (or outright teach) that attending church is required to be a successful Christian, that the more you attend, the better, and that no matter what else might be going on in your life, church attendance is the cure for what ails you. So if you just attend, everything will improve and get better.

This constant pressure has a lot of similarities with drug pushers, except that pastors are pushing the drug of religious performance and Sunday service attendance. They tell you that if life is not going as you think it should, God has something special He wants to tell you, and you can hear what that is … if you come to church. Pastors tell you that when life gets you down, you need to have people around you who can encourage and help you, and if you want this, you can get it by … coming to church. If you are dealing with sin and temptation, pastors tell you that God wants to empower you to defeat sin and the devil, and you can get empowered for this … at church. Church attendance is often peddled like snake oil: it is the miracle cure for all that ails you.

Beyond this, pastors often present their case just like a drug pusher tempts potential addicts. If you don't attend church at all, the invitation is just to "give it a try." They will invite you to a special service or event that is geared especially for people who do not attend church. Usually they will not take an offering at these events, and nothing offensive will be preached. "The first one's free!" Then, after they get you to try it out once, the offer is to become a regular user. You are reminded of how the event you attended made you feel. You are shown examples and told stories of how regular church attendance saved jobs, rescued marriages, delivered people from bondage, provided financial security, and helped raise kids to become lawyers and doctors.

Once people start using church regularly, the pressure is then added to become a bi-weekly user. Pastors say things like, "Nobody can survive on one meal a week. You need a mid-week pick-me-up. Try our Wednesday night fellowship, or a small-group Bible study." And if you start attending one of these, they up the ante and invite you to join the prayer group. Then the accountability group. Then volunteer for the youth outing. And then get involved with the choir. Before you know it, you are not only at a church activity twice on Sunday, but also on every night and two mornings each week, as well as during one full "retreat" weekend every quarter!

Just when you are on the verge of burning out, they invite you to stand up in church and share with everyone about how meaningful your life has become now that you are at church 26 hours every week. You accept, because by this time, you cannot "just say no." Besides, this opportunity to speak in front of the entire congregation might be the first step in becoming a pastor of the church or leading your own ministry! This recognition is what you have been praying for, and all your hopes and dreams are finally coming true.

You fail to realize that somewhere along the way you became

addicted to church services. And the pastors—either because they didn't know any better or because they needed you to help alleviate their own ministry addiction—pushed the drug of church attendance and service upon you. Many pastors are only too happy to allow their congregations to depend on church attendance, because attendance addictions fill the pews and the offering plates on Sunday morning. In fact, many pastors reinforce such behavior. In the minds of most church leaders, the "truly committed and faithful followers" of Jesus Christ are those who are at the church whenever the doors are open. I know that I felt this way as a pastor. I expected it of my elders.

Somewhere along the way, just as with any other drug, this addiction to church causes people to lose their relationships with neighbors, coworkers, unchurched friends, and even some family members. We only have time for church people and church activities, and even then we become so busy and frantic that we rarely have any time to get to know the people we serve alongside.

It is tragic.

We don't mean to do this, but sadly, most of us do not know any other way.

Yet this is not the way church is supposed to be. There is not a single verse in Scripture which says that attending church is an indication of spiritual health or that God is using you in mighty ways if you are busy with church activities. There is nothing of the sort anywhere in the Bible. Quite to the contrary, such a mentality reveals a deep misunderstanding of the purpose and function of the church. Pastors who teach and encourage such behavior not only enable this dependence, but have even become pushers, trying to get more and more people hooked on the drug of church services.

To break free, to destroy the dependence, to stop the enablement, pastors may have to do something drastic. It is not enough to simply tell people in the church service that there is more to following Jesus than showing up at a building for another service. In fact, the whole situation is quite ironic. People attend church to hear sermons about how attending church is not enough, and if they show up next week for church, they will hear part two of the sermon series on why attending church is not enough. It may be that the church needs to follow the example of drug and alcohol rehab centers and require that the people go "cold turkey." Cancel the Sunday services and see what happens.

If we really seek to let people follow Jesus into the love of God and love for other people, it is essential that we first help people break their drug addiction to church attendance and church involvement. In the book *Finding Church*, Brian Swan writes about his drug addiction to church attendance and how he found his way out of it. One of the first steps for breaking his addiction was the same step required of any addict: He had to admit he was addicted. Here is what he writes:

> Admitting I was an addict was the first step toward breaking free from the love of knowledge, and finding again the love of Jesus. For the first time in my spiritual life I was seeing Christ for who he is, not the knowledge fed from the pulpit and injected into me by every program the institution sold. Most of the people I hung around with were all knowledge-consuming drug addicts. The drug we ate, drank, snorted, and smoked together kept us all on a spiritual high and gave us a false sense of relationship and community. The institution did the job it was created to do. The system kept our butts in

the pews, our heads in the books, and us always looking for the next fix (or study). We were soulless, supporting a self-serving entity. As long as our addictions were fed, everything went smoothly. We were happy for every new fix, and the institution was happy to provide it.[5]

If church leaders and pastors want to help people truly follow Jesus, rather than some man-made religious construction of performance and control, we need to give the people the freedom to follow Jesus away from the Sunday morning church service and all its activities, and maybe we even need the courage to lead them away ourselves. Jesus is calling us to let His people go!

LET MY PEOPLE GO!

As a church leader, this idea is scary. When Jesus says, "Let My people go!" we look around at the buildings we have constructed, the programs we have built, and the prominence we have in our community, and we fear that if we let the people go, all that we have worked for will come crashing down. Though we sometimes say "If we build it, they will come," we also know that "They who come have built it." If we let them go, no one will be left to help us finish our grand plan for "reaching the world for Christ" and "becoming a beacon of light and hope in our city."

So when Jesus says, "Let My people go!" we say, "No! We need them. They are ours. They belong to us. They help us build

---

[5] See Brian Swan's chapter in Jeremy Myers, ed. *Finding Church: Stories of Leaving, Switching, and Reforming* (San Jose, CA: Civitas, 2012), 79-80.

our empire. They give us power and authority. If we let them go, we do not know what will happen."

Actually, we do know what will happen. If you cancel your church service, the outcome is easy to predict: Most of the members of your church will go down the street to another church and start attending there. Then you will get fired.

Nobody wants that. I don't want that. If you are a pastor or church leader, I do not want you to lose your income. I do not want you to get fired.[6] Similarly, if the only outcome of canceling a church service is that the people leave one church and start attending another, then nothing has been accomplished. The point of canceling a church service is not just so that people can start attending a different service. No, if we cancel a church service, it needs to be done with intention and purpose. People need to be told *why* it is being done, *what* their response can be, and *how* this drastic action will help them better follow Jesus into the world.

So although this chapter has been recommending that churches cancel their church services, it is unwise to do so without some preparatory steps. Before canceling everything all at once, some small, initial steps might be necessary. First, it would be wise for pastors and the church leaders to explain to the church what they are thinking of doing and why. Part of this process should place an emphasis on the fact that canceling the church service does not mean the church is shutting down. Rather, canceling the Sunday

---

[6] If you feel led to quit your job that is another matter (and it is a topic we will cover later).

service helps the church move outward into the world.

Second, it should also be emphasized that canceling the church service is not another program or gimmick to increase attendance. Instead, it is a genuine effort by the leaders of the church to show the people that church attendance is optional, and that there are other ways of following Jesus into the world. Sadly, there are many pastors and churches who would use the idea of canceling a church service to simply get more attention for themselves and their church in the community and somehow leverage the canceled service into a way to invite more people to church or get more people involved in church. I can hear it now, "Since there is no church next week, invite your neighbor out to a picnic, and tell them that the reason you can do this is because your church canceled its Sunday service. Then see if they want to join you in attending church the following week." If you are a church leader who wants to help your people follow Jesus into the world, do not fall for any temptation to use canceling your church service as a way to increase your attendance! Avoid such thinking at all costs. Such thinking is manipulative and seeks to gain more control over other people through the illusion of giving up control.

Third, if the church does want to cancel their service, it might be wise to start with something infrequent, such as one service per month. It would probably be too much of a shock to the church leadership and the church members if they went cold turkey from all church services all at once. The common experience of people who stop attending church is that there is an initial period of time where they feel guilty on Sunday morning for not going to church, and they often don't know what to do with themselves.

Sometimes they try to replace the Sunday service with something "religious," such as hosting a small fellowship in their home or having a family Bible study. A church may be able to help their people transition away from an attendance dependence by only canceling one service per month or at the most two.

The final small step that church leaders can take to help people follow Jesus into the world would be to make sure that *nothing* is scheduled to replace the canceled service. If the church service is canceled, the temptation will be to schedule something else in its place. But this temptation once again shows how deeply the church leaders want to remain in control of where the people go and what the people do on Sunday morning. Ironically, the greatest fear that church leaders have about canceling the church service is that the people will use the opportunity to go visit another church in town, and maybe they won't come back. But again, if the people are told in advance what the canceled church service is for, and why the church is doing it, this should not be a fear. And besides, even if people do visit another church, this also is no great threat, because other churches in town are not "the competition" but are just other expressions of the worldwide family of God. It's not about your church, but about the Kingdom … right?

So in advance, the people should be told in as many ways as possible that the church is canceling the service to show that church attendance is optional and that there are other ways of following Jesus into the world which do not require sitting in a building on Sunday morning. It should be emphasized that there will be plenty of opportunities down the road for serving and loving others like Jesus, so initially, all they should do is learn to get comfortable with the idea of not attending church. The people can sleep in, go golfing, take a hike in the woods, or enjoy a day with the family.

When that Sunday comes, the church doors should remain locked and a sign can be posted which says, "Church service canceled today. Enjoy your day and see you next week!" Canceling a church service, of course, should be done with purpose. It is to show the people what church is really all about.

PUT THE SERVICE BACK IN CHURCH SERVICE

Though you may begin by simply canceling one service per month, you will eventually want to cancel all of your church services. Why? To put real service back into the church service. The goal of canceling the Sunday service is not just to free up some time or give people a break, but to give people the time and freedom to *actually* love and serve others.

Let's look at this another way. Satan doesn't care too much if Christians faithfully attend church. The more services we have and the longer these services are, the more delighted he is. In fact, I think Satan loves Christians sitting in church more than he loves them sitting at home watching television. Why? Because sitting in church makes us feel righteous, holy, and obedient. Singing songs to God and listening to sermons helps us feel like we are worshipping God and doing what He wants. These religious activities make us feel good about our church involvement, even if we never accomplish the goal and mission of the church.

I am not saying that it would better to sit home and watch television. This is the not the reason God called us out of the world.

But neither did God call us out of the world so we could sit in a pew listening to a sermon. Church attendance is not the reason God called us out of the world. No, the one thing God wants is the one thing Satan doesn't. God wants followers of Jesus who actually follow Jesus into the world.

So the reason for canceling church services is to put service back into the church service. The reason for canceling church services is to get followers of Jesus off the warm, padded pews in church and out onto the cold, hard, concrete street corners of the world. Or maybe onto the sandy beaches. But you get the point. Canceling the church service is not a gimmick. It is not another program to tack on to the church as a way to get more people to come to church. Canceling the church service is not a church-growth strategy. No, it is the exact opposite. It is a church-death strategy. If you follow this suggestion to its logical conclusion, you will eventually have no church services at all, and this, frankly, is a death-knell for most churches. But in the process, we will truly learn to be the church. Canceling the church service is a way to get people out of the church building so they can actually love and serve the hurting and lonely people in the world. If this is truly what we want, we can begin by canceling the church service.

There is no one right way to do this. We have the freedom to be creative and flexible.

If you are not a church leader, you might feel the freedom to just quit attending church altogether. Though some will condemn you for doing so, there is no guilt or shame in it if you are following Jesus away from church attending so that you can love people in the world. Just take the plunge, be courageous, and be willing and ready for whatever Jesus has in store. Be warned though, the process of moving away from church attendance and finding God's way of loving people in the world usually takes at least 3-5 years; sometimes more. It is unlikely that you will stop attending church one week and will immediately find people to love and serve the following week.

No, if your experience is anything like that of the millions of people who have followed this path before you, once you stop attending the church service, you will enter one of the hardest times of your life. You will go through periods of guilt and doubt. You will lose most of your Christian friends. You might experience some sort of hardship in your life, your health, your family, or your job. Former Christian friends will tell you that these things are God's judgment upon you for leaving church. Do not believe them. This is God taking you through the Valley of the Shadow of Death to break you and mold you into a person who looks like Jesus. These experiences are necessary to show you what the lonely and hurting people all around you go through on a regular basis. These experiences teach you sympathy, empathy, patience, grace, mercy, long-suffering, forgiveness, and a whole host of other Christlike attributes which are necessary for the disciple of Jesus who follows Him to the gates of hell.

But one thing will be sure. After a few months of following Jesus outside the four walls of the church, you will likely experience more joy and freedom in your relationship with God than ever before. He will reveal Himself to you in ways you never thought possible. Your life with God will truly become a daily adventure. What used to drive you and concern you will fade away into insignificance, and the life with God which you have only read about in books will become a reality. Friendships will grow and flourish with people you would have previously shunned. You will find great peace in circumstances that would have terrified you before. And most of all ... you will know that you are loved.

This is not everyone's path. Many people are not yet ready to stop attending church. That is fine. If you are finding love, joy, fellowship, and intimacy with God in a traditional church setting, and you feel that you are able to show others in your neighborhood and community the genuine love of Jesus, then by all means, stay where you are!

Of course, if you are a pastor or a church leader, you may have no choice but to stay. At least for a while. Maybe you have been sensing God leading you away from traditional church and into a more relational and natural way of following Jesus. If so, there will be difficult steps which you must take to follow Jesus in such a way.

But if you want to stay in your current position, there are ways which you can help liberate yourself and the people you work with to find freedom and flexibility in following Jesus and loving others. But a word of warning is in order. I have said it before, but I will emphasize it again. The temptation will be for you to use the following suggestions as just another way to manipulate people and control them. Avoid such desires at all costs. These suggestions are not another way to increase attendance at church, help your congregation get noticed in the community, or help the people look to you more for leadership and guidance.

Nowhere in this process of helping people follow Jesus into the world should there ever be any mention of inviting people to church, getting them involved in a church program, or plugging people into a church ministry. If that is why you are thinking of canceling a church service, it would be better to not do it at all. If you are going to do any "training" at all on what people should do during the time that they usually attend church, make sure you emphasize that if they are going to develop genuine relationships with people around them, these relationships *cannot ever in any way* be based on the goal of inviting these people to church.

It should be mentioned that very early on in the relationship, the church-going people will be faced with a decision: they will be forced to choose between attending a church service or program and showing love to someone. You must give them the freedom and the permission to skip the church service so that they can love the person God has placed in their path. If you are not willing to grant people permission—your blessing even!—to do this, then canceling a church service to help people follow Jesus into the world should not be something you promote.

As people seek to follow Jesus into the world, their journey will be similar to that of a woman I know named Lynn.

THE STORY OF LYNN

Lynn was seeking to learn how to follow Jesus into the world and love others whom she met there. Though her and her family had lived in the neighborhood for several years, they had never really come to know their neighbors. When she began to look around at who God might have placed in her life to love, she met a Hispanic family on one side of her house who barely spoke English and whose children needed help with math and science. Being a former teacher, she offered to tutor them for free. A few weeks later, Lynn met a mom who lived across the street who was an atheist.

The two of them struck up a wonderful friendship as they found out they were both struggling with many of the same issues with their husbands and their children. They became a source of encouragement and joy for each other as they helped each other through their trials. But Lynn quickly found out that she was often forced to choose between going to church and loving the people whom God brought into her life. Whenever this happened, she made a conscious decision to always choose people over church.

One Sunday morning, as she was on her way to church, she saw a hitch-hiker who needed a ride across town. Lynn was already running late for church, and she had her three daughters in the car with her, so she felt a little nervous about picking up a strange man on the side of the road. But she believed that at that moment, helping this man was more important than getting to church to sit in a pew, sing some songs, and listen to a sermon. So she stopped, let the man climb in, and gave him a lift to where he needed to go. It took them about 25 minutes to get where they were going, and on the way they talked about life, God, family, and a variety of other topics.

When they arrived at their destination, Lynn gave the man a few bucks, for which he thanked her and went on his way. Lynn then turned around and drove home. She never "went to church" that day but told her girls on the drive home that though they did not make it to church that day, they had shared the love of Jesus with someone in need, and that *was* church. It was not long before Lynn and her family stopped attending church altogether so that they could focus on loving others in their neighborhood and town instead. The time, energy, and money which usually went toward church activities now became devoted to loving others like Jesus.

Lynn got some flak from some church members for her decision, and most of her extended family did not understand either. But she recently told me that she will never go back, for the love, freedom, joy, intimacy, and friendships that she now experiences with people all around her is greater than anything she ever had as a church-going Christian. She has followed Jesus into the world and in the process, found the reality of life with Jesus in a way she had never experienced in church. Lynn is living life with Jesus and others when she laughs with neighbors and cries with friends; when she buys beer at the grocery check-out line for soldiers behind her in line; when she provides meals and sits with a man who lost his wife; when she plays with the children of homeless families downtown; when she just loves anybody whom God places in her path. She does not go out seeking people to love but simply lives her life with her eyes and her heart wide open to the people around her.

I recently asked Lynn if she thought she could still do these things *and* attend church. She didn't even have to think about the answer. She adamantly said, "No!" When I asked her why, she said that the mind frame and mentality that church-goers must adopt keeps them from viewing people as Jesus views them and loving people in the way that relationships require. Here is what she said:

> Most churches teach that the most important thing in the life of a Christian is church attendance. They may not blatantly say it that way, but that is what is implied and practiced. But true relation-

ships and genuine love will always interfere with attending church. Always. Most Christians, when faced with the choice of loving others or going to church will choose going to church. No relationship can survive that choice.

Christians will often try to have their cake and eat it too by inviting the people they are trying to love to attend church with them. But the people who need our love most don't need church; they need love. They need to be shown that they are more important than attending a church service. And if a Christian is trying to show love to another person, inviting them to a church service is one of the quickest ways of destroying that friendship. Why? Because if the person says no, that they don't want to go to church, the Christian is forced to choose between the friendship and the church, and sadly, most Christians choose church.

I do not know if Lynn is right. I do not know that it is impossible to both attend church *and* love others in the world. I agree that what she describes happens all too often, but I am hopeful. I hope that there might be some creative and adventurous churches out there that truly and genuinely give people the freedom and flexibility to attend church if they find it helpful but to not show up when opportunities come along to develop relationships and love others like Jesus. But if this "both-and" way of living is going to happen, church leaders must model this in their own life. They must be willing to not show up for a church service on a moment's notice. They must be willing to not make people accountable for Sunday morning attendance. They must be willing to celebrate the fact that people don't show up for a Sunday service, because loving others like Jesus in the midst of life is a higher priority. They must be willing to accept the fact that money spent loving others instead of on a church building is money well-spent. Even saying this makes me realize that Lynn is probably right, that such a way of doing church is impossible. Imagine if the Senior Pastor just didn't show up for a Sunday service because he was helping a neighbor! Or if the worship leader skipped out because she was driving a homeless person across town! A typical church could not survive this sort of disruption. But I am hopeful that there might be churches out there that want to try.

PRACTICAL SUGGESTIONS

Are you up for the challenge? If you are looking for some ways to love others in your community, the opportunities are endless. But I am not going to provide any concrete, practical suggestions or ideas. Why not? Because there are not "Ten Steps to Loving Your Community Like Jesus." Furthermore, each situation is completely unique. I do not know you, your setting, the people in your church, or the people in your community. All of these things are factors that must be considered when we seek to move out of the church building to love others like Jesus.

Nevertheless, there are some general ideas I can provide to help you and your church move to the place where you can begin to love and serve others. Again, these are not things you *must* do to love others likes Jesus, but are simply some suggested ideas for things which could be done to help you or your group move out of your building and into loving relationships with people all around. The following ideas apply to large mega churches with giant buildings as well as small-group churches that meet in houses. Any size of building and any type of meeting can keep us from loving others like Jesus. So any step that helps us move outside the comfort zone of our buildings and meetings, and into the realm of love for others is a step toward following Jesus into the world.

First, if your church decides to do something together for the community, it is probably wise for this group to have several months where the church services are canceled and nothing at all is scheduled in their place. The initial goal of canceling a church service is to show people that it is okay to not attend church. Before people are led into a group event of loving others, they need to learn that they can also do these things on their own and that it is okay to live life among others and follow Jesus wherever He leads. If this initial step of canceling the church service and scheduling nothing in its place is not done, then nothing else should be done either. Any attempt at replacing a canceled church service with a church activity will simply be viewed as an alternative to attending church, which is not the goal at all. So the first step is simply to cancel one church service (or two) per month, and schedule nothing whatsoever in its place. Nothing!

After the canceled church service has been in place for several months (or even a year or longer), a church may want to do something as a group to love and serve the surrounding community. If a church group wants to do this, my suggestion is that they *not replace* the canceled Sunday service, but rather *cancel an additional service* each month. Eventually the goal would be to have relatively few "church services" in the church building, maybe only one per month (or less). When this is done, the schedule may look something like this:

First Sunday: Group Gathering in the Church Building

Second Sunday: Freedom to Stay Home, Live Life, and Love Others

Third Sunday: Group Service Event in the Community

Fourth Sunday: Freedom to Stay Home, Live Life, and Love Others

We have already talked about the days where Christians are given the freedom to just stay home and do whatever they want, so nothing more needs to be said about this. Initially, this might be one Sunday per month, and later expanded to two. Then at some point, the church could cancel a third Sunday service, and plan some sort of group service event in the community. Again— and I cannot emphasize this enough—the goal is *not* to do some sort of community outreach event so that you can invite people to church. Church attendance is not the goal and never should be the goal. The goal is to love others like Jesus with no strings attached. Ward off all attempts and desires to get people to come to church, as any hint of such things will completely ruin the sincerity of your love for others, and they will sense it.

If the church is only feeding homeless people to get them to come to church or to get the church's name in the newspaper so that other people come to church, then the church is not really showing love; it is simply trying to gain control over the lives of others and garner power and prominence for themselves in the community. So in whatever community service event you undertake, there should be no gospel tracts, no sermons, no Bible lessons, no singing, no prayer meetings, no pens with your church address printed on them, no business cards with the church website, and no calls to newspaper reporters to come see what is going on. There should be nothing of this sort. Just love.

But what if someone you are serving asks why you are doing what you are doing? Certainly, you can tell them that you love Jesus and you believe these are the sorts of things that Jesus would do. If they ask you if you are part of a church, it is fine to tell them. Just don't invite them to church. As a matter of fact, a better thing to say might be, "Yes, this is my church, right here, with you." After all, loving others like Jesus is a truer church than the brick building with the steeple down on the corner, right? If someone finds out you are a follower of Jesus and asks you to pray for them, you can. But don't make it religious or preachy. You are just there to love and serve.

Note that the suggested schedule above includes one Sunday per month as a time of corporate fellowship for encouragement, planning, preparation, training, brainstorming, teaching, and celebration. This gathering would be a time to praise God for what has been done in the previous month, and a time to hear about some of the things people have done and how God has been at work. There could also be a time of teaching, which does not just include theological and biblical insights, but also provides some practical ideas and concrete suggestions for areas of need and ministry in the wider community. People would be encouraged to use the Sunday mornings they have free to just look for people whom God places in their path to love and serve.

This one Sunday church service would be a time to announce the group community project that would be taking place later in the month and invite the people to come together for loving and serving the community. I believe that if this sort of church service structure and schedule were followed, it would not only transform our churches into true life-giving communities of faith and love, but would also revitalize the personal lives of the people in our churches. Rather than get overwhelmed with all the church activities and responsibilities, people would be able to put into practice on a daily and weekly basis what they have learned from Scripture.

So what sorts of things might your church do as a group in the community? Again, I am not going to give specific recommendations, but rather some general guidelines and principles. As your church is looking for ways to serve your community, the first thing to do is to look at the people you have in your congregation and see what types of people God has brought together in your group. What are their skills and interests? Then, it might also be a good idea to ask the people what sorts of needs they are aware of in the community. If we are looking for ways to love and serve others, God usually lays needs upon the hearts and minds of His people. You can get a good idea of what God might want your church to do by comparing the skills and interests of the people in the church with the needs of which they are aware in the community. Then go do these things.

Here is one other point of advice: when you seek to love and serve the community, the lower you go the better. I always find it odd how many churches claim that God has called them to minister to the business professionals and the political leaders in the city. While it is true that God loves the rich, the famous, and the powerful just as much as He loves the sick, the poor, and the homeless, most churches seem to gravitate toward the first group, while the ministry of Jesus seemed to place special emphasis on the second. So if you are going to follow Jesus in loving others, try to focus initially on the outcast, the neglected, and the despised. Again, this is not because God loves them more, but because this will help ward off the temptation to seek power and prominence in the community and allow us to focus on love for others.

Finally, if the leadership of a church was serious about reaching the people who don't come to church on Sunday, one good approach might be to find the places where these people are already gathered on a Sunday morning and go join them in what they are doing. When following this suggestion, you might end up tailgating at the football coliseum, fishing at the bass lake, or hiking in the mountains. I guarantee that if we genuinely participated in some of these things during the hours we were usually in church, more relationship building would take place in one month than what usually happens during an entire year of sitting in church.

GIVE PRESENCE

Such days of leadership-led church service in the community shows people that church is not about entering a brick building on Sunday morning, but having a tangible presence in our cities, towns, and neighborhoods. This is ultimately what living like Jesus is all about. We follow Jesus by being present among the people, not asking them to join us in what we are doing, but going to join them in their activities and events, being with them in their sorrow and pain, and participating with them in their laughter and joy.

Too many Christians are trying to escape the world when we should be entering more fully into it. Following Jesus is not about escape. We are not here on earth to say prayers, sing songs, study the Bible, and wait for the rapture. As long as we are on this earth, we have something to do, and that "something" is not sitting in a church building. We must love and serve. We must restore peace and joy. We must announce that the morning has come, the sun has risen, the exile is over. People must be shown that God is not mad, that the world is not all evil, and that the Kingdom is at hand. We must live lives of hope, restoration, and redemption. And the only way we can reveal such things is by being present with the people in the world.

But presence is not about going where the people are so we can preach on the street corner, sing Christian songs, or hand out bottles of water with Bible verses printed on them. Presence is not simply being *among* people. Presence is sharing life with people, spending time with them, being friends for the long haul. It's not about getting people to reform their lives so they can be accepted by us and *our* community. It is about us entering fully into their lives, hoping they will accept us into *their* community.

To do this, it is quite possible that we must change more than they. We must become more like them, rather than ask them to become more like us. According to Philippians 2, when Jesus entered this world, He emptied Himself of nearly everything which identified Himself as God and became fully human. He did not ask us to become more like God; He became more like us. As we enter into the world, we must do the same.

Where can you start? The possibilities are endless. Go to your local Chamber of Commerce or city website and get a community calendar as well as a list of civic organizations and community service events. Then be present at the community events and projects that sound interesting to you. Be an active, joyful, service-minded citizen in your city.

Or you could join activity-based clubs such as hiking clubs, book clubs, and tourist clubs. You could adopt a park and hang out there on a regular basis, cleaning and restoring it. You could hang out at a local bar or nightclub, getting to know the regulars, and blessing the owner with your business. You could participate in the tractor-pulling contest or the art festival. Just look around in the newspaper and on community bulletin boards for events that you can join.

However, there is one important key for learning to love and live like Jesus in your community. It is this: Don't trade one "To Do" list for another. Don't trade one checklist for another. Do not give up church activities and programs just to get involved in community activities and programs. I know I have suggested some of these above, but the actual activity I am proposing is much simpler. All we need to do is live our lives with the single goal of loving others.

As you stand in line at the grocery store, you might notice a solider suffering from PTSD, or an elderly person struggling with the technology of the self-checkout line. Can you help in some way? Maybe you'll see a young child trying to get his mother's attention as she texts on her phone. Can you play peek-a-boo with him for a minute and bring a smile to his face? Perhaps the man in front of you was rude to the cashier. Can you offer her a word of encouragement and praise when she checks you out?

Look at your neighbor's yard when you pull into your driveway. Rather than complain about their weeds or unraked leaves, can you offer to do some yardwork for them? Can you dance with your daughter when her favorite song comes on the radio? Make your husband's favorite meal? Do the dishes for your wife?

Do you see? It is not about adding things to our life "to do" but about adding love to what we are already doing. As we go about our day, seeking to love whomever God brings into our path, it is amazing to watch His love pour through us toward those who need it. It doesn't have to be much. But when you give up the two or three hours you used to spend in a building on Sunday morning, you can use some of this time to add love to your day as you interact with others.

By entering our community with the goal of loving others, we do not cancel the church service because attendance has dried up and the bills aren't getting paid. Rather, we cancel the service so we can actually go out and serve. We cancel the church service so we can go out into the community to see and share Jesus. We cancel our church services not because we are dying, but because we are living. We do this not because we've lost the war against sin, death, and the devil, but because we've won. We do not throw up our hands in defeat, run up a white flag, and huddle in our Bible studies and prayer meetings until the airlift arrives to take us home. No, we rise up out of the trenches, break through the locked gates and closed doors of our own church buildings, and enter fully into the world with the message of hope, love, forgiveness, restoration, reconciliation, healing, and redemption.

We cancel the church service so that we can truly serve. We cancel the church service, not so that we can give people other things to do, but so that we can free them up to live their life and add love to what they are already doing. This is how the church truly lives like Jesus in the world.

DISCUSSION QUESTIONS

1. What were your first thoughts when this chapter invited you to cancel your church service?

2. Why do you think Christians equate church attendance with faithfulness to God? Is this valid? Why or why not?

3. Can you think of a Bible verse or passage that instructs Christians to "go to church"? Though many cite Hebrews 10:25, what does this verse *actually* teach?

4. What are the four steps to wisely and respectfully canceling a church service?

5. What is the main goal for canceling the church service? What is the one goal you must NOT have in canceling your church service? Are we to just trade one "To Do" list for another, or one set of activities for another? How are we to live instead?

6. Read the story of Lynn again. Why does Lynn think it is impossible for people to attend church on Sunday and also have meaningful relationships with people outside of church?

7. If you could gain three more hours per week, how would you spend that time? (Don't try to be "spiritual" here! If you need more sleep, write it down!)

8. What would you think and how would you feel if someone told you that you could stop attending church on Sunday morning and accomplish the items from Question 2 instead? (Guess what? That's *exactly* what you *can* do!)

9. Do you think you would feel guilty for "missing church"? If so, recognize that this guilt does not come from God, but from the manipulation of religious obligation. Also recognize that "going to church" on Sunday morning is not the same thing as "being the church" in your day-to-day life. Do you think you can try this way of being church for three months? Or maybe a year? What do you think will happen if you do? What are your fears?

10. Name two people in your life who could benefit from you having three extra hours per week. (Yes, your kids and spouse count!) What would you do with them that would help them see they are loved?

CHAPTER 2

CUT ALL CHURCH PROGRAMS

"I would rather feel compassion
than know the meaning of it."

—Thomas Aquinas

Once you cancel your church services, the next logical step is to also cut your church programs. This chapter explains why and how, although the reasoning is quite similar to what we have seen in the previous chapter. Therefore, this chapter will be relatively short.

However, when I first sat down to write this chapter, it rapidly became extremely long—it was thousands upon thousands of words. I poured time and creative energy into the chapter for hours and hours. It took me weeks to write. When I finished, I read through the chapter and realized, much to my dismay, that I didn't believe a word of what I had written. I had written what I *used* to believe about church programs, yet didn't believe any longer.

So I cut the chapter. The entire thing. Every word. Gone. Kaput.

For a while, I was pretty upset. I had put a lot of time and energy into that chapter. It was disheartening to cut it all out.

When I told my wife about the setback, she just smiled and said, "That's great!"

I thought she wasn't listening, and so continued to bemoan what had happened. "All that work. All that time. All that energy. Wasted. Gone. Nothing to show for it."

She just smiled again and said, "Yes. Just like most church programs."

It then dawned on me what she was saying. Church programs use up vast amounts of time, energy, and resources. Every attempt at fixing a church program only adds to the wasted time, effort, and energy. The only real way to fix a church program is to cut it.

My wife then advised me to put the chapter back in, but with only one sentence. She suggested this sentence: "Do to your church programs what I did to all the words in this chapter: Cut them."

It was genius.

But I didn't quite have the courage to do that to this chapter, and frankly, most pastors probably do not have the courage to cut all their programs. But in something far less than what was originally written, let me try to explain why most (if not all) church programs should be cut.

THE REASON FOR PROGRAMS

Though the stated reason for most church programs is "to make disciples and evangelize the world," church programs rarely ever accomplish either of these goals. When you step back and really look hard at what most church programs do and why churches do them, it becomes painfully obvious that most church programs primarily function to keep church people busy and use up church funds. Church programs are there to keep church people involved in church functions so they feel like they are doing something in the Kingdom of God … even if they aren't.

I know this sounds harsh, but if you take almost any program of any church, you will see that this is true. The only way we can say that most church programs accomplish discipleship is if we define discipleship as sitting in a room learning more about the Bible. The only way we can say that most church programs accomplish world evangelism is if we define evangelism as praying for the lost and learning about all the evil in the world.

I am sorry to put it this way, but it is the truth. Study after study has shown that the vast majority of churches have less than 1% conversion growth per year, and when it comes to almost any biblical standard of discipleship (such as morality, ethics, or generosity) church-going Christians live no different than the rest of the world.[1] Yet worldwide, the church pours millions of hours and billions of dollars into church programs every single year.

Church programs make church people feel like they are actually accomplishing something, but in reality, the only real result of church programs is that they consume vast amounts of time and money. Church programs give the appearance of progress, but they are some of the most inefficient ways of living in the Kingdom of God. Worst of all, these programs drain Christians of

---

[1] New churches tend to have about 10% conversion growth while older, more established churches hover around 0%. So while the majority of churches have less than 1% conversion growth, the national average is about 3% when you consider the total number of Christians attending church.

energy and time that they could be using to love and serve others in the world.

THE CHURCH INEFFICIENT

In an era where people are doing everything possible to cut budgets and become energy efficient, the church must do the same. Of course, I'm not talking about the electric bill and "going green." No, the biggest area of waste, fraud, and abuse within the church is with the money and time that people give to church programs. Are we truly getting a significant return on our vast expenditures in these areas?

Though church programming and activities are never about the numbers but about faithfulness in love and service toward others, it is nevertheless helpful to look at some actual numbers so that we might see the inefficiency and ineffectiveness of church programming. Though I do not believe numbers tell us much about church, let us look at some numbers anyway, just for the sake of argument. Bear with me in a little foolishness (2 Cor 11:1).

Studies show that most churches average only three conversions per year for every 100 people who attend. These are *actual* conversions, not just people transferring from one church to another. Based on this statistic, let's look at how much money and time churches spend on average to gain these three conversions.

It is estimated that the cost of running a church is about $1,700 each year for each regular attendee. This number is within ballpark range for small churches and mega churches. A church of 50, with a building and one pastor, costs about $85,000 per year to operate. A mega-church, like Rick Warren's Saddleback Community Church, costs $34 million for 20,000 in weekend attendance. Most churches are "within the ballpark" of this $1,700 figure.

If the average church gets three conversions for every 100 people, and the average church expense for 100 people is about $170,000, then the average expense per conversion is over $50,000. Yes, a lot more is going on in church than just evangelism, and a lot of the money is spent on discipleship training for those who believe. But still, if one of the goals of discipleship is evangelism, then properly discipled believers should result in a greater number of conversions. But it is not.

So the question becomes: Would you support a non-profit organization which had the stated goal of "evangelizing the lost" but spent over $50,000 for each convert? I don't know about you, but I would have difficulty supporting such a ministry, especially if they had been doing this for 2,000 years and their effectiveness had become worse over time.

But what about those church programs that do not "cost" anything—at least, not according to the church budget? Well, aside from the money, consider the cost in time. Though many people spend only an hour or so in church activities per week, others spend much more. Some, such as the church staff, devote 60 hours or more each week to church activities. Of course, this is their job so maybe we cannot count them. But on average, a typical church member spends about three hours per week on church activities. This includes spending time in the Sunday morning service, but does not count the time they spend getting ready for church, driving to church, and going out for lunch after church.

Nor does it include personal Bible study or prayer time during the week. This is time they actually spend in the church building or in a designated church program.

Three hours per week isn't a whole lot when you realize that the average person watches that much television every single night of the week, but still, it appears that even these few hours spent on "church" accomplish very little. Three hours per person per week results in about 150 hours per year. So 100 people spend about 15,000 hours per year on "church activities." Again, if we take the average conversion rate of three conversions per 100 people, this means that about 5,000 hours go into each conversion. When you realize that a full-time job (40 hours per week) fills 2,000 hours per year, each conversion takes two-and-a-half years of work.

So again I ask, if you were supporting a missionary who had one conversion every two-and-a-half years, would you continue to support that missionary?

I know; conversions aren't everything. We have all heard the stories about missionaries who labor for forty years without seeing a single conversion. But these stories are often followed up with the fact that when a new missionary arrives on the scene, they reap a harvest of hundreds or thousands of conversions in the first few years of work. This is not because they figured out something that their predecessor did not, but because the faithful missionary who served forty years without seeing a single conversion had prepared the soil, planted the seed, and watered the ground for the new missionary who reaped the harvest. So statistically, we do expect the *average* conversion rate for missionaries to be much higher than one conversion every two-and-a-half years.

Is all of this time and money really a good investment? Possibly. No price is too high for the single soul, and a lot more goes on in the typical church than just seeking conversions. For that $1,700 and 150 hours per person, the people who attend also get friends, fellowship, encouragement, support, guidance, and spiritual education. So maybe it is all worth it.

But what if there were a more efficient way of providing all of this, while at the same time seeing more people become followers of Jesus? Again, while numbers are not that important, the question must nevertheless be asked: If $50,000 and 5,000 hours is worth it to see one person saved, wouldn't it be even better if we found a more efficient way of spreading the gospel and expanding the Kingdom of God on earth?

Yes, but how?

Some people think the answer is that we just need more and better training. But is this the answer? Or is all this training just another way of wasting time and money?

ALWAYS AT TRAINING, NEVER TRAINED

A vast majority of church programming involves training people to do the things God calls us to do. In an effort to get more converts, make more disciples, and help people become more like Jesus, we pour large amounts of time and money into programs that train people. In fact, most church programs consist of little more than sitting in a room getting trained. Very rarely is there a church program that does not begin with training, involve training, or consist entirely of training. We think this is natural, normal, and necessary. After all, if people are not properly trained, they cannot properly serve. At least, this is what we are trained to think.

Church leaders love to train church people, and church people love to receive training. We hold evangelism training, discipleship training, Bible study training, and small group training. I have even seen churches that offer trainer training. They don't call it that, but essentially they are training people to train people.

What happens with all this training? We end up stuck on the train tracks. All this training produces lots of noise, lots of commotion, and even lots of movement. Generally, all this commotion and noise is all in one direction. This isn't all bad, of course. Such training helps a church get from Point A to Point B. But it doesn't do a whole lot of good for people who aren't on the train. And if someone tries to get off the train at times and places other than the designated stops, well, things get very messy and very painful very quickly.

So training is helpful, but only to a point. How often have you talked with people in the church who say they want to go out and serve people, but they simply don't have the time? But as you talk further, you find out they are involved in two or three different Bible studies and prayer groups, and they attend various training sessions and seminars throughout the year. They are convinced that while they will *eventually* help and serve people, right now they just need a little bit more training.

This is the problem and the trap of training. Once we tell people that they need to be trained to teach, or minister, or lead, or serve, many people believe that all they need to be used by God is a little more training. Then a little more. And after that, some more. Once they get on this track, it becomes nearly impossible to get off. People view training programs as open doors, as opportunities that were sent from God. They hear a sermon about evangelism, and they feel in their heart that they want to evangelize. But they don't know how. So they pray about it, and at just that time, they hear an announcement at church which invites them to "Evangelism Training." So they figure that before they go evangelize, it would be a smart move to get some training.

You have probably had this happen to you. You see a need in a certain part of town, but you are too nervous to start doing something because of some issue you wouldn't know how to handle, a certain type of person you might meet, or a question you might encounter. And just about that time, you discover a seminar, conference, or training session that will meet that specific need in your life. So you pay the $129 and go sit for a weekend in a room with a couple hundred other people who are there to get the same training.

Afterwards, you go home, but that is where it ends. If your experience is like most, the training never actually results in *doing* anything, but only convinces you of your need to read more books, study the Bible more, and attend more trainings. You spent dozens of hours and the $129 registration fee (and maybe even more on hotel and food costs and a few books from the "Resource Table") and ended up no closer to actually accomplishing what God laid on your heart to do in the first place. Often, training serves as a substitute for actual service.

Training Christians to do "Christian" things is a favorite activity of church leaders and church people alike, and in fact, the training often serves as an easy substitute for the actual thing the Christian is being trained to do.

DON'T REWORK IT. KILL IT!

So what does Jesus want us to do? Can we change the programs, training seminars, and conferences so they are more effective? Can we rework and tweak them so they become more efficient? Such changes might be possible, but I doubt it is worth the effort. Church programs are like Government programs: They can be reworked, but only with lots of time, energy, and money being wasted, with the end results possibly worse than where we started. Attempting to retool a program is nearly always more damaging to the church and the people in the program than just flat-out canceling the program.

So I suggest that just as with the church service, church programs simply be cut. Cancel them all. Kill them quickly. Yes, every single one. No more Sunday school. No more Bible studies. No more training seminars. No more evangelism outreach. No more Food Bank. Wipe the slate clean. Clear out the church calendar. Delete all the bulletin announcements. Trash all the flyers in the foyer.

But ... but ...

Yes. Now you are getting the picture.

Ideally, you leave it that way. Just as canceling the church service allows the people to move out of the building and into loving relationships with other people, so also, cutting all church programs—every single one!—also gives people the time and energy to love and serve others in their town and community as Jesus intends. They don't need programs to do this. They definitely don't need training. All they need is time, energy, and the freedom to follow Jesus. By cutting all church programs, we give these things to them and we trust Jesus to lead the people where He wants.

I know it's difficult. But it must be done.

If you want to help the people in your church actually follow Jesus into the world, you must take the hard but critical step of cutting, canceling, and killing every church program. Hold nothing back. You will, of course, want to inform the church in advance what will be happening, and will definitely want to have the full support of the elders or governing board before taking this step. But don't skip it, and don't go half-way. Church programs cannot be "reworked" while they are ongoing.

Think of your church programs like Hostess. During the week I wrote this paragraph, it was announced on the news that Hostess Twinkies, Cupcakes, Ding Dongs, and Ho-Hos will be returning to the shelves in the summer of 2013 after filing for bankruptcy, shutting its doors, and laying off all of its workers in early 2012. When Hostess shut down, it declared that its current operating structure did not allow it to remain in business. And so it closed.

Now, over a year later, the Hostess brand is being resurrected so that people all over the world can once again kill themselves slowly with delicious cream-filled food items.

The analogy isn't so good, but the point is clear. Just as Hostess could not simply "rework" its operating plan and remain in business, so also, most church programs cannot simply be reworked. They must die before they can rise again. Death precedes resurrection.

If a local church wants to have programs, they must begin by killing all their current programs. Every single one must die so that there is no favoritism and so that every program can be equally modified in a way that supports the true goals and mission of the Kingdom of God, and in a way that gives time, energy, and freedom back to the people of God who are seeking to follow Jesus into the world.

Another reason to kill all the current church programs is because any new church program is going to be stamped with an expiration date. If death always precedes resurrection, then before any new program is birthed, it must plan for death. The creation of a program must begin with a plan to kill the program.

Generally, programs are designed to last. And they do last. They perpetually exist until the original vision and need for the program has long since died. The program becomes "untouchable" even though it drains the church of valuable volunteers and resources. So before any new programs are started, their death should be scheduled right in. Not only will this ensure that no program exists "until Christ returns," but it will force those who design the program to think carefully about the purpose and goals of the program.

The reason most programs exist forever and ever without really accomplishing anything is because the goals and purposes were unclear from the beginning. If nobody knows what exactly is supposed to happen, there is no way to know when it has been accomplished. But if the program has a specific goal, it is much easier to accomplish and complete. For example, many churches have a program with the goal of "feeding the hungry." That program, clearly, will never be fully accomplished. And it's a good program, so we can't just kill it, can we? Not really. But what if the "feed the hungry" program did die, and instead, we started a program to "feed Jim Handley's family for six months or until he finds a job"? With this sort of a program, the church has a specific need in mind, and the process of meeting this need helps build relationships, and hopefully, helping Jim Handley find a job is a by-product of this program. And of course, the death of the program is built right in. If, after six months, Jim still doesn't have a job, the "program" can be reassessed, but it should not be blindly continued. If he does find a job, then the successful program can be celebrated, and the families who were providing food for Jim and his family can take their exciting success into new directions.

In this way, the impending death of a program acts like the impending death of our own life. It gives us a sense of urgency to get done what needs to get done. It forces us to set priorities, and to reevaluate as things progress. Impending death demands innovation and creativity. Also, as we saw with the Jim Handley example, if the program is successful, we can rejoice at a program well lived. But if the program fails, it is still okay, because we learned in the process, we developed relationships along the way, and though the ultimate goal was not achieved, at least the program is not a dead corpse that we have to drag around to every calendar and budget meeting for the next decade.

So programming your programs for death is the key to successful programs. Needs change, people change, and programs must change too. And changing a program is much easier to do if they all die.

Of course, you may have noticed that what is being described doesn't sound like much of a "program" at all. At least, not the way most churches define "church programs." Helping a man find a job and feeding his family while he searches is not a "program." That's just love. That's just serving people. Anybody can do that. We don't need committees, budget meetings, planning coordinators, bulletin announcements, sign-up sheets, and pleas for volunteers for such a thing. All we need is a few people who see a need and are willing to take a few steps to meet that need.

Right!

It turns out that when we kill all our fancy and expensive church programs (which really weren't accomplishing anything anyway) to make the church programs more relational, effective, and short-term, the end result is not a "program" at all, but simply people loving and serving other people. And that looks a lot like Jesus!

Though I understand that most churches and church leaders are not comfortable with cutting and canceling all church programs across the board, when we kill them so we can resurrect them with small, concrete, easily-accomplished goals in mind, and with expiration dates stamped on them from the very start, we find that the programs we develop don't look much like programs at all, but more like people simply loving and serving other people. This understanding helps church people and church leaders transition away from formal programs and into giving the freedom and flexibility of allowing others to love others like Jesus.

Ah, but what about the training? Certainly part of discipleship is training, right?

Well again, just as loving and serving others looks a lot like Jesus, we can also learn to train Christians in the same way Jesus trained His disciples. Jesus performed "on the job" training.

ON THE WAY PROGRAMS

Jesus never really did any formal training with His disciples. Sure, He taught and instructed them, but it was almost always on the way to something Jesus was going to do, or as a debriefing for something He had already done. Eventually, He just kicked them out the door with a pair of shoes and a shirt, and said, "Come back in a few weeks and we'll talk about how it went" (Luke 10).

Let's look at how the church could train in similar ways.

First, churches should never offer anything that consists only of training. All training should be done on the way to the actual service that will be performed. If Jesus taught evangelism training today, He would announce the training in church, in the bulletin, and on the website. Then, on the night of the training, when everyone arrives, He would say, "Ok. We're all here? Good. There's a van out back. Let's pile in. We're going to go downtown and hang out with drug addicts. I'll tell you what you need to know on the way." Then afterwards, on the drive home, He would host a Q&A session.

We can plan our programs in similar ways. There should never be a program without training, but there should also never be training without a majority of the time doing the actual thing for which we are being trained. Any program or training that does not include actually loving or serving someone in some way should not be done.

This leads to the second point, which is about the types of programs the church should have. All programs should be designed to help, serve, or love other people. I love to study the Bible, but the absolute last thing the church needs right now is more Bible studies. The same goes for prayer meetings; we don't need more prayer meetings. If you are planning a program, don't make it a Bible study or a prayer meeting. Most Christians already know more than we need to know about the Bible to obey it, and we need to start being answers to our own prayers before we pray about it more. If you want to study Scripture and pray about what you are going to do, fit these elements in while you are on the way to love or serve somebody.

Finally, as we saw above, since all programs are being designed to meet specific needs of specific people, it is logical to design the programs to meet small, achievable needs of a few people, rather than the vast, insurmountable needs of a few million people. In this way, we don't need big budgets or huge crowds of volunteers to accomplish our programs. All we need are a few people to meet the specific needs of a few people. This is relational and loving in ways that large programs with big budgets can never be.

Some people say you need large groups of people to accomplish big things for God, but I do not believe this is true at all. Jesus said that the Kingdom of Heaven is like a mustard seed. And while He goes on to say that the mustard seed grows into a large tree so that even the birds can sit in the branches (Matt 13:31-32), I don't think Jesus meant that some Kingdom activities begin in small ways, but others begin huge. No, He was saying that everything within the Kingdom of God begins in small ways, but the outcome is huge. What seems insignificant and tiny has immense results.

So it is with anything that we do in the Kingdom of God. We don't need large budgets, planning committees, and petitions for money. We shouldn't have to twist the arms of unwilling recruits.

All we need is for a few people to see a specific need, and then reach out with the love of Jesus in a relational way to help the person in front of them. This is how Jesus went about His ministry, and it is how we as the followers of Jesus can go about ours. This approach liberates the people to create their own personal programs and follow Jesus wherever, however, whenever, and to whomever He leads.

If none of this sounds like a church program after all, that's because it isn't. It's just people serving and loving other people. This may not look much like "church," but it certainly looks like Jesus.

FREEDOM TO FOLLOW JESUS

Ultimately, it's all about freedom to follow Jesus wherever He leads. Church programs restrict our time, creativity, and freedom. Church programs do not allow us to follow Jesus in some new direction, because we have prior obligations to attend or work at a church program that never ends.

Think about a church program that you or your children are involved with. How much time is spent at this program? Add to this the time you spend preparing lessons, getting dressed, and driving back and forth. Now think of all the people you have had to say "No" to this week when they make requests on your time and energy.

If you could choose between the program and the people, which would you choose? Doesn't it look more like Jesus to abandon the church programs so that you could follow Jesus in loving and serving the people He is bringing into your life?

When viewed from this perspective, canceling your church programs is not a sad thing. It should be celebrated, for it frees you up to have more time for friends and family. It shouldn't create guilt; it should increase your joy, freedom, and sense of satisfaction in your life as a Christian. Canceling church programs gives you a brand new start in your journey with God. And I promise ... you will be surprised at how enjoyable and refreshing it can be to follow Jesus into the world.

DISCUSSION QUESTIONS

1. Have you ever gone to training of any kind for a Christian program? If so, what was it? Looking back, how valuable was it? Did you put into practice what you learned?

2. If you attend Bible studies, have you ever used the knowledge you gained from these studies to actually help someone in a tangible way? (Quoting Bible verses and correcting someone's theology doesn't count). If so, what happened and how did your Bible knowledge help? If not, what does this tell you about endless Bible studies?

3. If you attend prayer meetings, have you ever taken it upon yourself to be the answer to your own prayers? If so, what happened? If not, what does this tell you about many prayer meetings?

4. If you have children, would you want them to do nothing but sit at home and listen to you teach them about how to live life, or would you want them to go out and put into practice the things they have seen and heard from you? Do you think God feels similarly?

5. What do you think about the statistics in this chapter about how much it costs to convert one person to Christianity? Do you think there might be a better way?

6. Which is easier? To attend a program and then go home, or to actually go out and love people like Jesus? Do you think this has anything to do with why most Christians are content to attend program after program after program?

7. Which has the potential to make you feel more joy and satisfaction as a follower of Jesus? To attend a program and then go home, or to actually go out and love people like Jesus?

CHAPTER 3

IT'S THE END OF THE CHURCH AS WE KNOW IT

*"The more organization you bring to church life,
the less life it will contain."* —Wayne Jacobsen

As you have read this book and considered the two simple (but incredibly difficult) ideas it proposes of cutting church services and church programs, you have probably thought to yourself, "If I do this, it will kill my church!"

The truth is that it probably will. But these two suggestions of canceling your church service and cutting your church programs will not kill the church; rather, will only kill the church *as you know it.* What will rise in its place is far more beautiful, far more loving, and far more Christlike than anything you know now. As I argued in *The Death and Resurrection of the Church,* the end of the church as we know it will give way to the life of the church as it was meant to be.[1] The end of church as you know it will look different for church members and church leaders, so let me say a few words to each group.

---

[1] Jeremy Myers, *The Death and Resurrection of the Church* (Dallas, OR: Redeeming Press, 2013).

FOR CHURCH MEMBERS

If you are a church member, I want to encourage you to not make waves or cause problems at your particular church over these sorts of issues. Many people in church—especially church leaders—are not ready to hear or even consider the outrageous and shocking idea of canceling a church service and cutting church programs. In the minds of most, the church cannot exist without these things, and if you suggest otherwise, you will not be seen as a person who is trying to help the church rise up and follow Jesus into the world, but will be viewed as a threat and may even get yourself labeled as a heretic and apostate.

So if you are a church member and you want to take some of the steps suggested in this book, just quietly and peacefully take them. You do not need to draw attention to yourself, nor do you need to try to get others to follow you away from the church service and church programs. This will be seen as divisive. Instead, just slowly extract yourself from involvement in church services and church programs.

Know that you will probably feel guilty about this for a while, but this is the guilt that comes from abandoning a man-made religion, not the guilt that comes from disobeying God. You are not leaving the church service and programs to abandon God but exactly the opposite! You are separating yourself from church activities and functions *which keep you* from serving God so that you can truly begin to love and serve others like Jesus.

Along with the guilt, there will be the temptation to replace the absent church activities with some other sort of activity or meeting. Do your best to resist this temptation. It does no good if you give up the activity of a church service only to take up the activity of a Bible study and prayer meeting in your home. No, the way to follow Jesus into the world is literally to follow Jesus into the world. The "into the world" part is crucial. You must get up and just go someplace. Any place. Find an activity that you enjoy doing. Maybe it is horseback riding. Or camping. Or going to quilt shows. Or shopping. Or watching car races. Maybe it is not something fun, but it is something that must be done, such as running errands, getting the car fixed, taking the dog to the vet, exercising at the gym, or mowing your lawn. These are the things that allow you to get into the world.

Once you are in the world, you need to start looking for Jesus, as well as ways to be Jesus to others. You must believe that Jesus led you there for a purpose. That there is somebody He wants you to love. Somebody who needs help. Somebody who needs encouragement. Somebody who needs a friend. As you go out into the world, look for ways that you can love and serve other people like Jesus.

You will be absolutely shocked at how often and how frequently Jesus brings hurting and lonely people into your life. You will develop friendships you never knew were possible. You will have conversations about life and God that you never had before. You will see people's lives touched. You will see healing, hope, and love return to your own life. You will experience joy again.

But it is not all laughter, sunshine, and rainbows. Though this way of following Jesus is unlike anything you may have experienced "in church," there are potholes in the road as well. The first thing that will probably happen is that you will lose most of your Christian friends. When someone leaves church, church-going people feel rejected, condemned, and threatened, and so they will often reject, condemn, and threaten in return. Expect this to happen, but do not defend yourself or condemn them in return. Just because you have been led away from church as it is traditionally practiced does not mean that others will be led by God in similar ways at similar times. If you are pressed for an explanation of your actions, it is best to simply say something along the following lines, "I have not abandoned God or the church in any way. I am simply following Jesus to the best of my ability by loving and serving the people whom God brings into my life." They will not understand and will quote Scripture at you (most likely Hebrews 10:25), and eventually, most of your Christian friends will no longer have time for you. This is fine though, because only now are you beginning to see what unchurched people see when they look at the church.

Another thing that will probably happen to you is that you will experience some sort of great tragedy, pain, hardship, or trial in life. When this comes, make sure you have it clearly fixed in your mind that this tragedy *did not come from God.* Despite what some Christians will tell you, this tragedy in your life is not God's punishment upon you for leaving church. No, quite the contrary, it is either just life happening to you, or it is the devil trying to chase you back into the arms of church attendance and religious obligation. The devil gets scared when people leave the church to follow Jesus into the world because now we are truly entering his territory and he sees us as a threat. But know this: wherever this trial and tragedy came from, God will use it to accomplish His good purpose in you. He will use the pain to mold you and shape you into the image of Jesus. He will use it to help you understand the hopeless experience of most people in the world. He will use this tragedy to grow your faith and help you see other people as He sees them. This pain and tragedy is one of the hardest parts about leaving traditional church, but it is essential if we are going to follow Jesus into the world—to the very gates of hell—and rescue the people who are there.

As you come out of this tragedy (or a whole string of them), you will begin to see with greater clarity the situation that this world is in and the lostness and loneliness of people all around, and your heart will develop the heart of God for them. You will develop friendships with people you never would have befriended before. You will find the faith and courage to go places you never would have gone before. You will find yourself in deep conversations with strangers about the most amazing spiritual questions and issues. You will look around one day and find yourself serving and loving people in real and tangible ways. You will be shocked, amazed, and overjoyed. The love of the Father, the life of Jesus, and the power of the Spirit will be flowing in you and through you in ways you had always heard and read about, but had never before experienced.

As mentioned earlier, the entire process described in the previous few paragraphs will not happen in a month or two. From my own experience and by observing this process in the lives of others or through conversations I have had with them, this process seems to take about 3-5 years. But when you get a ways down this road of truly following Jesus outside the four walls of church performance and religious obligation, when you have been liberated from the business of church services and church programs, you will never want to go back. So enjoy the journey. Let Jesus take you along for the ride. When you trust Him in this way, your life will never be the same.

FOR CHURCH LEADERS

If you are a church leader or a pastor, hopefully you have just read what I wrote to church members and do not feel threatened by it. Hopefully you see that I am not trying to destroy your ministry or your church. I have no desire to pull people away from you, but only to help encourage people to follow after Jesus wherever He leads. I believe you want the same thing. And is it so bad if people connect with Jesus outside the four walls of the church, and learn to love and serve others in real and tangible ways even though they may no longer attend your church? I hope you would agree that this is not a bad thing.

In fact, I hope you would want this very thing for yourself. Much of what I have written to church members above can be true for you as well. Many church leaders are getting burned out by "ministry" because there is too much pressure, too much stress, too much activity, and very little ever seems to get accomplished. Maybe you too have begun to feel the tug of Jesus upon your life and heart to follow Him away from the church. Maybe as you have read this book, you have felt the desire to try to implement some of what has been suggested in your church so that you can help lead others into the life of following Jesus into the world.

Before you do so, however, make sure you count the cost and understand what the consequences might be. Taking some of the steps in the previous chapters may result in the loss of your job. So if you have the courage to take some of these steps, it might also be wise to begin looking for an alternative source of income. The church system, as it functions today, *requires* the regular and frenetic activity of the Sunday morning church service and a full plate of daily programming. If you lead your church to give these up, do not be surprised if this church system rises up against you and takes away your salary. You might be wise to read the writing on the wall and transition into a bi-vocational or "tentmaking" position at your church as part of this process of leading the church out of the building and into the world. When you are not taking a salary, the church system has much less power.

This is what I did, and it is one reason why I am no longer a pastor today. I used to be a full-time pastor, and as I started to learn about some of the things I have written in this book (and in my other books), I began to look for alternative sources of income. My plan was to stop taking a salary but continue to pastor a church. I won't get into all the details, but the plan didn't work out so well. Nevertheless, I am glad that God brought me to where I am now, and I am excited to see what the next step in this amazing journey might be. I am not saying that your journey will be identical to mine, but you do need to know that following Jesus in some of the ways suggested above will lead to drastic changes in your own life and ministry, and you need to be prepared for things that do not turn out as planned.

Is it possible to lead your church into canceling the services and cutting the programs and still maintain your job? I think it might be possible. It didn't work that way for me (at least, not yet), but it might work out for you. But notice that even if you lose your salary as a pastor, you do not stop being a pastor. In fact, I have found that not getting paid to be a pastor has opened up more opportunities and avenues to actually serve, tend, care for, and shepherd people than I ever had as a paid pastor. Being a pastor does not require a salary; it just requires a heart willing to love, serve, protect, and guide other people who are on the same journey as you.

People sometimes ask me if I will ever become a pastor again. I know what they are asking, but I always try to explain that in many ways, I am more of a pastor now than ever before. But then I go on to say that I know that this is not what they meant, and so I try to answer the question they asked, which is "Will I ever again accept a position in a traditional church setting?" I always say that it would take a unique church to hire me as their pastor. In fact, as can be guessed from the previous chapters in this book, hiring me as the pastor of a church would probably be the death-knell for the church (at least, the church as they know it).

The church that might hire me would have to be the kind of church where they knew that the pastor may not show up for the Sunday service. It would be a church where the people knew that the Sunday service is completely optional, that they didn't have to show up either. It would be a church where the people knew that inviting other people to church is discouraged. It would be a church where the people knew that rather than tithe to the church, we preferred they use their money for hospitality in their home, or to buy food, clothes, and tarps to pass out to the homeless. It would be a church where rather than ask people to open their homes for another small group Bible study, we ask them to open their homes to abused children and battered women.

These sorts of actions would destroy the typical church, but these are the sorts of actions, behaviors, and mindsets I would encourage in the people who attended any church I pastored. So as you can see, the chance of me getting hired by any church is extremely small. And as a church leader, if you adopt some of these same mindsets, the chances of you maintaining your employment at your church are also extremely small. Nevertheless, it *is* possible, and I think that the chances are improving every day. I believe that there is a worldwide movement of God upon the hearts and minds of His people to call all of us to move out into the world with acts of love and service toward people who have traditionally been despised, rejected, and condemned by the church. If, in God's perfect planning, a group of people who have this heart of God are perfectly paired with a pastor and other church leaders who also have this heart, then God can move mightily and beautifully in such a setting to lift up the name of Jesus and advance the Kingdom of God on earth. Maybe you and your church are the congregation that will show the rest of us the way to do this, to cancel our services and cut our programs so that as the Body of Christ we can move out into the world to touch others with the love of Christ.

Are you ready? I hope so, because I am eager to see the church rise up in all the glory and radiance of the Father, with the power of the Spirit, going forth in the love and service of Jesus Christ. I cannot wait to see the end of the church as we know it so that we can finally see the resurrection of the church as it was meant to be.

CONCLUSION

I know that this book has generated some strong feelings and ideas in your heart and mind. You might have felt depressed at some of what I wrote, and maybe even angry. In fact, as I teach and share some of these things with other Christians, I have found that many church-going Christians feel that they have lots of *real* friends at church, engage in *real* ministry, and are making a *real* difference in the world.

If that is how you feel, then you should go ahead and disregard everything I have written in this book. Although I would encourage you to try one thing before you completely reject everything I have written. I invite you to stop attending all church services and programs for three months, just to see what happens. During this time, ask God to bring people into your life to love and serve in tangible ways.

If the ideas of this book are wrong, at the end of three months, you will have realized that what you had in your church services and church programs was more enjoyable and effective than following Jesus in freedom outside the church, and you can easily return and pick back up where you left off.

Yet you might find the opposite to be true. You might find, first of all, that the "real relationships" you thought you had at church were not so real after all. Most church "relationships" are only held together as long as people attend church. Church "friendships" tend to disintegrate once one person stops attending. If this is what happens, how *real* were these relationships in the first place?

Second, you might discover that Jesus leads you in some exciting directions, helping you love others like He does. You might see that He shows up in tangible ways in your life that you have only dreamt of before. You might gain the satisfaction and significance in your walk with God that you have always longed for.

The risk of leaving the church service and church programs is inconsequential when compared to the surpassing greatness of the potential reward. You have nothing to lose. Leave the church service and programs behind to follow Jesus into the great unknown. It will be the greatest adventure of your lifetime.

DISCUSSION QUESTIONS

1. Canceling your church service and programs may seem like the death of your church. But there is a biblical principle that "Death always precedes resurrection." So if you want the church to rise in glory and power, what does it need to do?

2. Does this chapter encourage church members to complain about how their church is run and criticize the leaders for not following some of the ideas in this book? What does this chapter encourage members to do instead?

3. If you stop attending the church service, does this mean you have abandoned the church or forsaken God? What does it *actually* mean? Therefore, is there any reason to feel guilty for not attending church on Sunday morning?

4. How will Jesus show up in this world as you seek to follow Him wherever He leads? Where are the sorts of places and people in which He can be found?

5. Will following Jesus outside the four walls of "Sunday morning church" be easy? Will you possibly be criticized and condemned by other Christians? How can you respond?

6. Some have described the process of experiencing church in a new way as a detoxification process. How long does this chapter suggest that this process can take? Are you ready to be patient as the Spirit works to lead you down this difficult path?

7. If you are a church leader and you try to implement some of the changes of this book, you will likely lose your job or position in the church. Are you ready for that? But note that such a loss might be liberating as well. How might it be liberating to no longer have to worry about church services and programs? (You should also read the other books in the "Close Your Church for Good" book series, as they provide further ideas about how to follow Jesus into the world.)

8. If you think the ideas of this book are wrong, why do you think this? If you like the ideas of this book, why do you think some Christians might find them dangerous? If you are unsure, are you willing to take the three-month challenge suggested in the conclusion? Try it and see where God leads!

ABOUT JEREMY MYERS

Jeremy Myers is an author, blogger, podcaster, and Bible teacher. Much of his content can be found at RedeemingGod.com, where he seeks to help liberate people from the shackles of religion. He lives in Oregon with his wife and three beautiful daughters.

If you appreciated the content of this book, would you consider recommending it to your friends and leaving a review on Amazon? Thanks!

JOIN JEREMY MYERS AND LEARN MORE

Take Bible and theology courses by joining Jeremy at
RedeemingGod.com/join/

Receive updates about free books, discounted books,
and new books by joining Jeremy at
RedeemingGod.com/read-books/

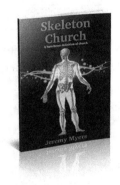

SKELETON CHURCH: A BARE-BONES DEFINITION OF CHURCH (PREFACE TO "THE CLOSE YOUR CHURCH FOR GOOD" BOOK SERIES)

The church has a skeleton which is identical in all types of churches. Unity and peace can develop in Christianity if we recognize this skeleton as the simple, bare-bones definition of church. But when we focus on the outer trappings—the skin, hair, and eye color, the clothes, the muscle tone, and other outward appearances—division and strife form within the church.

Let us return to the skeleton church and grow in unity once again.

REVIEWS FROM AMAZON

My church gathering is struggling to break away from traditions which keep us from following Jesus into the world. Jeremy's book lends encouragement and helpful information to groups like us. –Robert A. White

I worried about buying another book that aimed at reducing things to a simple minimum, but the associations of the author along with the price gave me reason to hope and means to see. I really liked this book. First, because it wasn't identical to what other simple church people are saying. He adds unique elements that are worth reading. Second, the size is small enough to read, think, and pray about without getting lost. –Abel Barba

In *Skeleton Church*, Jeremy Myers makes us rethink church. For Myers, the church isn't a style of worship, a row of pews, or even a building. Instead, the church is the people of God, which provides the basic skeletal structure of the church. The muscles, parts, and flesh of the church are how we carry Jesus' mission into our own neighborhoods in our own unique ways. This eBook will make you see the church differently. –Travis Mamone

This book gets back to the basics of the New Testament church—who we are as Christians and what our perspective should be in the world we live in today. Jeremy cuts away all the institutional layers of a church and gets to the heart of our purpose as Christians in the world we live in and how to affect the people around us with God heart and view in mind. Not a physical church in mind. It was a great book and I have read it twice now. –Vaughn Bender

The Skeleton Church … Oh. My. Word. Why aren't more people reading this!? It was well-written, explained everything beautifully, and it was one of the best explanations of how God intended for church to be. Not to mention an easy read! The author took it all apart, the church, and showed us how it should be. He made it real. If you are searching to find something or someone to show you what God intended for the church, this is the book you need to read. –Ericka

Purchase the Paperback
Purchase the eBook

THE DEATH AND RESURRECTION OF THE CHURCH (VOLUME 1 IN THE "CLOSE YOUR CHURCH FOR GOOD" BOOK SERIES)

In a day when many are looking for ways to revitalize the church, Jeremy Myers argues that the church should die.

This is not only because of the universal principle that death precedes resurrection, but also because the church has adopted certain Satanic values and goals and the only way to break free from our enslavement to these values is to die.

But death will not be the end of the church, just as death was not the end of Jesus. If the church follows Jesus into death, and even to the hellish places on earth, it is only then that the church will rise again to new life and vibrancy in the Kingdom of God.

REVIEWS FROM AMAZON

I have often thought on the church and how its acceptance of corporate methods and assimilation of cultural media mores taints its mission but Jeremy Myers eloquently captures in words the true crux of the matter—that the church is not a social club for do-gooders but to disseminate the good news to all the nooks and crannies in the world and particularly and primarily those bastions in the reign of evil. That the "gates of Hell" Jesus pronounces indicate that the church is in an offensive, not defensive, posture as gates are defensive structures.

I must confess that in reading I was inclined to be in agreement as many of the same thinkers that Myers riffs upon have influenced me also—Walter Wink, Robert Farrar Capon, Greg Boyd, NT Wright, etc. So as I read, I frequently nodded my head in agreement. –GN Trifanaff

The book is well written, easy to understand, organized and consistent thoughts. It rightfully makes the reader at least think about things as ... is "the way we have always done it" necessarily the Biblical or Christ-like way, or is it in fact very sinful?! I would recommend the book for pastors and church officers; those who have the most moving-and-shaking clout to implement changes, or keep things the same. –Joel M. Wilson

Absolutely phenomenal. Unless we let go of everything Adamic in our nature, we cannot embrace anything Christlike. For the church to die, we the individual temples must dig our graves. It is a must read for all who take issues about the body of Christ seriously. –Mordecai Petersburg

Purchase the eBook
Purchase the Paperback

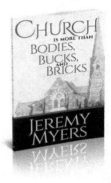

CHURCH IS MORE THAN BODIES, BUCKS, & BRICKS (VOLUME 3 IN THE "CLOSE YOUR CHURCH FOR GOOD" BOOK SERIES)

Many people define church as a place and time where people gather, a way for ministry money to be given and spent, and a building in which people regularly meet on Sunday mornings.

In this book, author and blogger Jeremy Myers shows that church is more than bodies, bucks, and bricks.

Church is the people of God who follow Jesus into the world, and we can be the church no matter how many people we are with, no matter the size of our church budget, and regardless of whether we have a church building or not.

By abandoning our emphasis on more people, bigger budgets, and newer buildings, we may actually liberate the church to better follow Jesus into the world.

REVIEWS FROM AMAZON

This book does more than just identify issues that have been bothering me about church as we know it, but it goes into history and explains how we got here. In this way it is similar to Viola's *Pagan Christianity*, but I found it a much more enjoyable read. Jeremy goes into more detail on the three issues he covers as well as giving a lot of practical advice on how to remedy these situations. –Portent

This book surprised me. I have never read anything from this author previously. The chapters on the evolution of the tithe were eye openers. This is something that has bothered me for years in the ministry. It may be truth that is too expensive to believe when it comes to feeding the monster. –Karl Ingersoll

Since I returned from Africa 20 years ago I have struggled with going to church back in the States. This book helped me not feel guilty and has helped me process this struggle. It is challenging and overflows with practical suggestions. He loves the church despite its imperfections and suggests ways to break the bondage we find ourselves in. –Truealian

Jeremy Meyers always writes a challenging book ... It seems the American church (as a whole) is very comfortable with the way things are ... The challenge is to get out of the brick and mortar buildings and stagnant programs and minister to the needy in person with funds in hand to meet their needs especially to the widows and orphans as we are directed in the scriptures. –GGTexas

Purchase the eBook
Purchase the Paperback

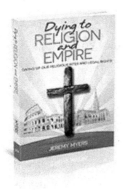

DYING TO RELIGION AND EMPIRE (VOLUME 4 IN THE "CLOSE YOUR CHURCH FOR GOOD" BOOK SERIES)

Could Christianity exist without religious rites or legal rights? In *Dying to Religion and Empire*, I not only answer this question with an emphatic "Yes!" but argue that if the church is going to thrive in the coming decades, we must give up our religious rites and legal rights.

Regarding religious rites, I call upon the church to abandon the quasi-magical traditions of water baptism and the Lord's Supper and transform or redeem these practices so that they reflect the symbolic meaning and intent which they had in New Testament times.

Furthermore, the church has become far too dependent upon certain legal rights for our continued existence. Ideas such as the right to life, liberty, and the pursuit of happiness are not conducive to living as the people of God who are called to follow Jesus into servanthood and death. Also, reliance upon the freedom of speech, the freedom of assembly, and other such freedoms as established by the Bill of Rights have made the church a servant of the state rather than a servant of God and the gospel. Such freedoms must be forsaken if we are going to live within the rule and reign of God on earth.

This book not only challenges religious and political liberals but conservatives as well. It is a call to leave behind the comfortable religion we know, and follow Jesus into the uncertain and wild ways of radical discipleship. To rise and live in the reality of God's Kingdom, we must first die to religion and empire.

REVIEWS FROM AMAZON

Jeremy is one of the freshest, freest authors out there— and you need to hear what he has to say. This book is startling and new in thought and conclusion. Are the "sacraments" inviolate? Why? Do you worship at a secular altar? Conservative? Liberal? Be prepared to open your eyes. Mr. Myers will not let you keep sleeping!

For all free-thinkers, for all who consider themselves "spiritual," for all who have come out or are on the way out of "Babylon," this is a new book for you! Treat yourself, buy this book and enjoy it! –Shawn P. Smith

Jeremy Myers is one or the most thought provoking authors that I read, this book has really helped me to look outside the box and start thinking how can I make more sense of my relationship with Christ and how can I show others in a way that impacts them the way that Jesus' disciples impacted their world. Great book, great author. –Brett Hotchkiss

Purchase the eBook
Purchase the Paperback

CRUCIFORM PASTORAL LEADERSHIP (VOLUME 5 IN THE "CLOSE YOUR CHURCH FOR GOOD" BOOK SERIES)

This book is forthcoming in early 2017.

The final volume in the *Close Your Church for Good* book series look at issues related to pastoral leadership in the church. It discusses topics such as preaching and pastoral pay from the perspective of the cross.

The best way pastors can lead their church is by following Jesus to the cross!

This book will be published in early 2020.

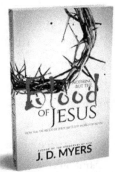

NOTHING BUT THE BLOOD OF JESUS: HOW THE SACRIFICE OF JESUS SAVES THE WORLD FROM SIN

Do you have difficulties reconciling God's behavior in the Old Testament with that of Jesus in the New?

Do you find yourself trying to rationalize God's violent demeanor in the Bible to unbelievers or even to yourself?

Does it seem disconcerting that God tells us not to kill others but He then takes part in some of the bloodiest wars and vindictive genocides in history?

The answer to all such questions is found in Jesus on the cross. By focusing your eyes on Jesus Christ and Him crucified, you come to understand that God was never angry at human sinners, and that no blood sacrifice was ever needed to purchase God's love, forgiveness, grace, and mercy.

In *Nothing but the Blood of Jesus*, J. D. Myers shows how the death of Jesus on the cross reveals the truth about the five concepts of sin, law, sacrifice, scapegoating, and bloodshed. After carefully defining each, this book shows how these definitions provide clarity on numerous biblical texts.

Building on his previous book, 'The Atonement of God', the work of René Girard and a solid grounding in the Scriptures, Jeremy Myers shares fresh and challenging insights with us about sin, law, sacrifice, scapegoating and blood. This book reveals to us how truly precious the blood of Jesus is and the way of escaping the cycle of blame, rivalry, scapegoating, sacrifice and violence that has plagued humanity since the time of Cain and Abel. 'Nothing but the Blood of Jesus' is an important and timely literary contribution to a world desperately in need of the non-violent message of Jesus. –Wesley Rostoll

So grateful to able to read such a profound insight into the Bible, and the truths it reveals, in this new book by Jeremy Myers. When reading both this book and the Atonement of God, I couldn't help but feel like the two disciples that walked with Jesus after His resurrection, scripture says that their eyes were opened...they knew Him... and they said to one another, 'Did not our heart burn within us while He talked with us on the road, and while He opened the Scriptures to us?'

My heart was so filled with joy while reading this book. Jeremy you've reminded me once more that as you walk with Jesus and spend time in His presence, He talks to you and reveals Himself through the Scriptures. –Amazon Reader

Purchase the eBook
Purchase the Paperback

THE ATONEMENT OF GOD: BUILDING YOUR THEOLOGY ON A CRUCIVISION OF GOD

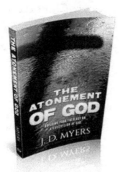

After reading this book, you will never read the Bible the same way again.

By reading this book, you will learn to see God in a whole new light. You will also learn to see yourself in a whole new light, and learn to live life in a whole new way.

The book begins with a short explanation of the various views of the atonement, including an explanation and defense of the "Non-Violent View" of the atonement. This view argues that God did not need or demand the death of Jesus in order to forgive sins. In fact, God has never been angry with us at all, but has always loved and always forgiven.

Following this explanation of the atonement, J. D. Myers takes you on a journey through 10 areas of theology which are radically changed and transformed by the Non-Violent view of the atonement. Read this book, and let your life and theology look more and more like Jesus Christ!

REVIEWS FROM AMAZON

Outstanding book! Thank you for helping me understand "Crucivision" and the "Non-Violent Atonement." Together, they help it all make sense and fit so well into my personal thinking about God. I am encouraged to be truly free to love and forgive, because God has always loved and forgiven without condition, because Christ exemplified this grace on the Cross, and because the Holy Spirit is in the midst of all life, continuing to show the way through people like you. –Samuel R. Mayer

If you have the same resolve as Paul, to know nothing but Jesus and Him crucified (2 Cor 2:2), then this book is for you. I read it the first time from start to finish on Father's Day ... no coincidence. This book revealed Father God's true character; not as an angry wrathful God, but as a kind loving merciful Father to us. Share in Jeremy's revelation concerning Jesus' crucifixion, and how this "vision" of the crucifixion (hence "crucivision") will make you fall in love with Jesus all over again, in a new and deeper way than you could imagine. Buy a copy for a friend—you won't want to give up your copy because you will want to read it again and again until the Holy Spirit makes Jeremy's revelation your revelation. –Amy

This book gives another view of the doctrines we have been taught all of our lives. And this actually makes more sense than what we have heard. I myself have had some of these thoughts but couldn't quite make the sense of it all by myself. J.D. Myers helped me answer some questions and settle some confusion for my doctrinal views. This is truly a refreshing read. Jesus really is the demonstration of who God is and God is much easier to understand than being so mean and vindictive in the Old Testament. The tension between the wrath of God and His justice and the love of God are eased when reading this understanding of the atonement. Read with an open mind and enjoy! –Clare Brownlee

Purchase the eBook
Purchase the Paperback

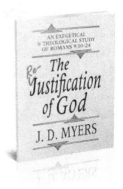

THE RE-JUSTIFICATION OF GOD: A STUDY OF ROMANS 9:10-24

Romans 9 has been a theological battleground for centuries. Scholars from all perspectives have debated whether Paul is teaching corporate or individual election, whether or not God truly hates Esau, and how to understand the hardening of Pharaoh's heart. Both sides have accused the other of misrepresenting God.

In this book, J. D. Myers presents a mediating position. Gleaning from both Calvinistic and Arminian insights into Romans 9, J. D. Myers presents a beautiful portrait of God as described by the pen of the Apostle Paul.

Here is a way to read Romans 9 which allows God to remain sovereign and free, but also allows our theology to avoid the deterministic tendencies which have entrapped certain systems of the past.

Read this book and—maybe for the first time—learn to see God the way Paul saw Him.

REVIEWS FROM AMAZON

Fantastic read! Jeremy Myers has a gift for seeing things from outside of the box and making it easy to understand for the rest of us. The Re -Justification of God provides a fresh and insightful look into Romans 9:10-24 by interpreting it within the context of chapters 9-11 and then fitting it into the framework of Paul's entire epistle as well. Jeremy manages to provide a solid theological exegesis on a widely misunderstood portion of scripture without it sounding to academic. Most importantly, it provides us with a better view and understanding of who God is. If I had a list of ten books that I thought every Christian should read, this one would be on the list. –Wesley Rostoll

I feel the author has spiritual insight to scripture and helps to explain things. I would recommend any of his work! –Uriah Scott

I loved this book! It made me cry and fall in love with God all over again. Romans is one of my favorite books, but now my eyes have been opened to what Paul was really saying. I knew in my heart that God was the good guy, but J. D. Meyers provided the analysis to prove the text. I have been examining all the "proofs" about reformed theology because I was attracted to the message, but couldn't go all the way down the TULIP path, because it did not resonate in my heart that God who is Holy would love imperfectly. I believed Holy trumped Sovereignty, yet, I believe in the sin message, wrath of God, the Gospel and Jesus and decided that I was a "middle of the road" person caught between two big Theologies (the Big C and A). Now, I get it. I can with great confidence read the difficult chapters of Romans, and my furrowed brow is eased. Thank you, J. D. Myers. I love God, even more and am so grateful that his is so longsuffering in his perfect love! Well done. –Treinhart

Purchase the eBook

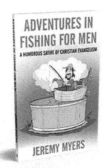

ADVENTURES IN FISHING FOR MEN

Adventures in Fishing for Men is a satirical look at evangelism and church growth strategies.

Using fictional accounts from his attempts to become a world-famous fisherman, Jeremy Myers shows how many of the evangelism and church growth strategies of today do little to actually reach the world for Jesus Christ.

Adventures in Fishing for Men pokes fun at some of the popular evangelistic techniques and strategies endorsed and practiced by many Christians in today's churches. The stories in this book show in humorous detail how little we understand the culture that surrounds us or how to properly reach people with the gospel of Jesus Christ. The story also shows how much time, energy, and money goes into evangelism preparation and training with the end result being that churches rarely accomplish any actual evangelism.

REVIEWS FROM AMAZON

I found *Adventures in Fishing For Men* quite funny! Jeremy Myers does a great job shining the light on some of the more common practices in Evangelism today. His allegory gently points to the foolishness that is found within a system that takes the preaching of the gospel and tries to reduce it to a simplified formula. A formula that takes what should be an organic, Spirit led experience and turns it into a gospel that is nutritionally benign.

If you have ever EE'd someone you may find Myers' book offensive, but if you have come to the place where you realize that Evangelism isn't a matter of a script and checklists, then you might benefit from this light-hearted peek at Evangelism today. –Jennifer L. Davis

Adventures in Fishing for Men is good book in understanding evangelism to be more than just being a set of methods or to do list to follow. –Ashok Daniel

<u>Purchase the eBook</u>

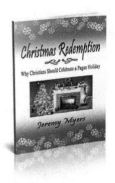

CHRISTMAS REDEMPTION: WHY CHRISTIANS SHOULD CELEBRATE A PAGAN HOLIDAY

Christmas Redemption looks at some of the symbolism and traditions of Christmas, including gifts, the Christmas tree, and even Santa Claus and shows how all of these can be celebrated and enjoyed by Christians as a true and accurate reflection of the gospel.

Though Christmas used to be a pagan holiday, it has been redeemed by Jesus.

If you have been told that Christmas is a pagan holiday and is based on the Roman festival of Saturnalia, or if you have been told that putting up a Christmas tree is idolatrous, or if you have been told that Santa Claus is Satanic and teaches children to be greedy, then you must read this book! In it, you will learn that all of these Christmas traditions have been redeemed by Jesus and are good and healthy ways of celebrating the truth of the gospel and the grace of Jesus Christ.

REVIEWS FROM AMAZON

Too many times we as Christians want to condemn nearly everything around us and in so doing become much like the Pharisees and religious leaders that Jesus encountered. I recommend this book to everyone who has concerns of how and why we celebrate Christmas. I recommend it to those who do not have any qualms in celebrating but may not know the history of Christmas. I recommend this book to everyone, no matter who or where you are, no matter your background or beliefs, no matter whether you are young or old. –David H.

Very informative book dealing with the roots of our modern Christmas traditions. The Biblical teaching on redemption is excellent! Highly recommended. –Tamara

Finally, an educated writing about Christmas traditions. I have every book Jeremy Myers has written. His writings are fresh and truthful. –Retlaw "Steadfast"

This is a wonderful book full of hope and joy. The book explains where Christmas traditions originated and how they have been changed and been adapted over the years. The hope that the grace that is hidden in the celebrations will turn more hearts to the Lord's call is very evident. Jeremy Myers has given us a lovely gift this Christmas. His insights will lift our hearts and remain with us a long time. –Janet Cardoza

I love how the author uses multiple sources to back up his opinions. He doesn't just use bible verses, he goes back into the history of the topics (pagan rituals, Santa, etc.) as well. Great book! –Jenna G.

Purchase the eBook

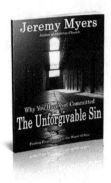

WHY YOU HAVE NOT COMMITTED THE UNFORGIVABLE SIN: FINDING FORGIVENESS FOR THE WORST OF SINS

Are you afraid that you have committed the unforgivable sin?

In this book, you will learn what this sin is and why you have not committed it. After surveying the various views about blasphemy against the Holy Spirit and examining Matthew 12:31-32, you will learn what the sin is and how it is committed.

As a result of reading this book, you will gain freedom from the fear of committing the worst of all sins, and learn how much God loves you!

REVIEWS FROM AMAZON

This book addressed things I have struggled and felt pandered to for years, and helped to bring wholeness to my heart again. –Natalie Fleming

A great read, on a controversial subject; biblical, historical and contextually treated to give the greatest understanding. May be the best on this subject (and there is very few) ever written. – Tony Vance

You must read this book. Forgiveness is necessary to see your blessings. So if you purchase this book, [you will have] no regrets. –Virtuous Woman

Jeremy Myers covers this most difficult topic thoroughly and with great compassion. –J. Holland

Good study. Very helpful. A must read. I like this study because it was an in depth study of the scripture. –Rose Knowles

Excellent read and helpful the reader offers hope for all who may be effected by this subject. He includes e-mails from people, [and] is very thorough. –Richie

Wonderful explication of the unpardonable sin. God loves you more than you know. May Jesus Christ be with you always. –Robert M Sawin III

Excellent book! Highly recommend for anyone who has anxiety and fear about having committed the unforgivable sin. –William Tom

As someone who is constantly worried that they have disappointed or offended God, this book was, quite literally, a "Godsend." I thought I had committed this sin as I swore against the Holy Spirit in my mind. It only started after reading the verse about it in the Bible. The swear words against Him came into my mind over and over and I couldn't seem to stop no matter how much I prayed. I was convinced I was going to hell and cried constantly. I was extremely worried and depressed. This book has allowed me to breathe again, to have hope again. Thank you, Jeremy. I will read and re-read. I believe this book was definitely God inspired. I only wish I had found it sooner. –Sue

Purchase the eBook
Purchase the Paperback

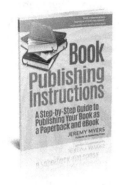

BOOK PUBLISHING INSTRUCTIONS: A STEP-BY-STEP GUIDE TO PUBLISHING YOUR BOOK AS A PAPERBACK AND EBOOK

The dirty little secret of the publishing industry is that authors don't really need publishing companies any longer. If you want to get published, you can!

This book gives you everything you need to take your unfinished manuscript and get it into print and into the hands of readers. It shows you how to format your manuscript for printing as a paperback and preparing the files for digital eReaders like the Kindle, iPad, and Nook.

This book provides tips and suggestions for editing and typesetting your book, inserting interior images, designing a book cover, and even marketing your book so that people will buy it and read it. Detailed descriptions of what to do are accompanied by screenshots for each step. Additional tools, tips, and websites are also provided which will help get your book published.

If you have a book idea, you need to read this book.

REVIEWS FROM AMAZON

I self-published my first book with the "assistance" of a publishing company. In the end I was extremely unhappy for various reasons

… Jeremy Myers' book … does not try to impress with all kinds of "learned quotations" but gets right to the thrust of things, plain and simple. For me this book will be a constant companion as I work on a considerable list of books on Christian doctrines. Whether you are a new aspiring author or one with a book or so behind you, save yourself much effort and frustration by investing in this book.
–Gerrie Malan

This book was incredibly helpful. I am in the process of writing my first book and the info in here has really helped me go into this process with a plan. I now realize how incredibly naive I was about what goes into publishing a book, yet instead of feeling overwhelmed, I now feel prepared for the task. Jeremy has laid out the steps to every aspect of publishing step by step as though they were recipes in a cook book. From writing with Styles and using the Style guide to incorporating images and page layouts, it is all there and will end up saving you hours of time in the editing phase.
–W. Rostoll

Purchase the eBook
Purchase the Paperback

THE LIE — A SHORT STORY

When one billion people disappear from earth, what explanation does the president provide? Is he telling the truth, or exposing an age-old lie?

This fictional short story contains his televised speech.

Have you ever wondered what the antichrist will say when a billion people disappear from planet earth at the rapture? Here is a fictional account of what he might say.

Purchase the eBook for $0.99

JOIN JEREMY MYERS AND LEARN MORE

Take Bible and theology courses by joining Jeremy at
RedeemingGod.com/join/

Receive updates about free books, discounted books,
and new books by joining Jeremy at
RedeemingGod.com/read-books/